Ecclesiastes

Life Under the Sun

JOHN A. STEWART

General Editor: Roque Albuquerque, Ph.D.

Lamplighters International is a Christian ministry that helps individuals engage with God and His Word and equips believers to be disciple-makers.

For additional information about Lamplighters ministry resources, contact:

Lamplighters International
771 NE Harding Street, Suite 250
Minneapolis, MN USA 55413
or visit our website at
www.LamplightersUSA.org

Product Code Ec-NK-2P

ISBN 978-1-931372-42-8

CONTENTS

How to Use This Study   5

What is an Intentional Discipleship Bible Study?   7

Introduction   11

1   Life is Meaningless   13
    (Ecclesiastes 1)

2   Pleasure Doesn't Satisfy   19
    (Ecclesiastes 2)

3   A Time for Everything   25
    (Ecclesiastes 3)

4   The Sacrifice of Fools   31
    (Ecclesiastes 4–5)

5   Work Doesn't Satisfy   37
    (Ecclesiastes 6)

6   True Righteousness   43
    (Ecclesiastes 7)

7   Who Is Wise?   49
    (Ecclesiastes 8)

8   Time and Chance   55
    (Ecclesiastes 9)

9   Risk and Reward   61
    (Ecclesiastes 10)

10 Living Without Fear   67
    (Ecclesiastes 11)

11 The Purpose of Life   73
    (Ecclesiastes 12)

Leader's Guide   79

Final Exam   _____ _____   106

Open House   _____ _____

Appendix   117

How to Use This Study

What Is Lamplighters?

Lamplighters is a Christian ministry that helps individuals engage with God and His Word and equips believers to be disciple-makers. This Bible study, comprising eleven individual lessons, is a self-contained unit and an integral part of the entire discipleship ministry. When you have completed the study, you will have a much greater understanding of a portion of God's Word, with many new truths that you can apply to your life.

How to study a Lamplighters Lesson

A Lamplighters study begins with prayer, your Bible, the weekly lesson, and a sincere desire to learn more about God's Word. The questions are presented in a progressive sequence as you work through the study material. You should not use Bible commentaries or other reference books (except a dictionary) until you have completed your weekly lesson and met with your weekly group. Approaching the Bible study in this way allows you to personally encounter many valuable spiritual truths from the Word of God.

To gain the most out of the Bible study, find a quiet place to complete your weekly lesson. Each lesson will take approximately 45–60 minutes to complete. You will likely spend more time on the first few lessons until you are familiar with the format, and our prayer is that each week will bring the discovery of important life principles.

The writing space within the weekly studies provides the opportunity for you to answer questions and respond to what you have learned. Putting answers in your own words, and including Scripture references where appropriate, will help you personalize and commit to memory the truths you have learned. The answers to the questions will be found in the Scripture references at the end of each question or in the passages listed at the beginning of each lesson.

If you are part of a small group, it's a good idea to record the specific dates that you'll be meeting to do the individual lessons. Record the specific dates each time the group will be meeting next to the lesson titles on the Contents page. Additional lines have been provided for you to record when you go through this same study at a later date.

The side margins in the lessons can be used for the spiritual insights you glean from other group or class members. Recording these spiritual truths will likely be a spiritual help to you and others when you go through this study again in the future.

Audio Introduction

A brief audio introduction is available to help you learn about the historical background of the book, gain an understanding of its theme and structure, and be introduced to some of the major truths. Audio introductions are available for all Lamplighters studies and are a great resource for the group leader; they can also be used to introduce the study to your group. To access the audio introductions, go to www.LamplightersUSA.org.

"Do You Think?" Questions

Each weekly study has a few "do you think?" questions designed to help you to make personal applications from the biblical truths you are learning. In the first lesson the "do you think?" questions are placed in italic print for easy identification. If you are part of a study group, your insightful answers to these questions could be a great source of spiritual encouragement to others.

Personal Questions

Occasionally you'll be asked to respond to personal questions. If you are part of a study group you may choose not to share your answers to these questions with the others. However, be sure to answer them for your own benefit because they will help you compare your present level of spiritual maturity to the biblical principles presented in the lesson.

A Final Word

Throughout this study the masculine pronouns are frequently used in the generic sense to avoid awkward sentence construction. When the pronouns he, him, and his are used in reference to the Trinity (God the Father, Jesus Christ, and the Holy Spirit), they always refer to the masculine gender.

This Lamplighters study was written after many hours of careful preparation. It is our prayer that it will help you "… grow in the grace and knowledge of our Lord and Savior Jesus Christ. To Him be the glory both now and forever. Amen" (2 Peter 3:18).

What Is an Intentional Discipleship Bible Study?

The *Next Step* in Bible Study

The Lamplighters Bible study series is ideal for individual, small group, and classroom use. This Bible study is also designed for Intentional Discipleship training. An Intentional Discipleship (ID) Bible study has four key components. Individually they are not unique, but together they form the powerful core of the ID Bible study process.

1. Objective: Lamplighters is a discipleship training ministry that has a dual objective: (1) to help individuals engage with God and His Word and (2) to equip believers to be disciple-makers. The small group format provides extensive opportunity for ministry training, and it's not limited by facilities, finances, or a lack of leadership staffing.

2. Content: The Bible is the focus rather than Christian books. Answers to the study questions are included within the study guides, so the theology is in the study material, not in the leader's mind. This accomplishes two key objectives: (1) It gives the group leader confidence to lead another individual or small group without fear, and (2) it protects the small group from theological error.

3. Process: The ID Bible study process begins with an Open House, which is followed by a 6–14-week study, which is followed by a presentation of the Final Exam (see graphic on page 8). This process provides a natural environment for continuous spiritual growth and leadership development.

4. Leadership Development: As group participants grow in Christ, they naturally invite others to the groups. The leader-trainer (1) identifies and recruits new potential leaders from within the group, (2) helps them register for online discipleship training, and (3) provides in-class leadership mentoring until they are both competent and confident to lead a group according to the ID Bible study process. This leadership development process is scalable, progressive, and comprehensive.

OVERVIEW OF THE LEADERSHIP TRAINING AND DEVELOPMENT PROCESS

There are three stages of leadership training in the Intentional Discipleship process: (1) leading studies, (2) training leaders, and (3) multiplying groups (see appendix for greater detail).

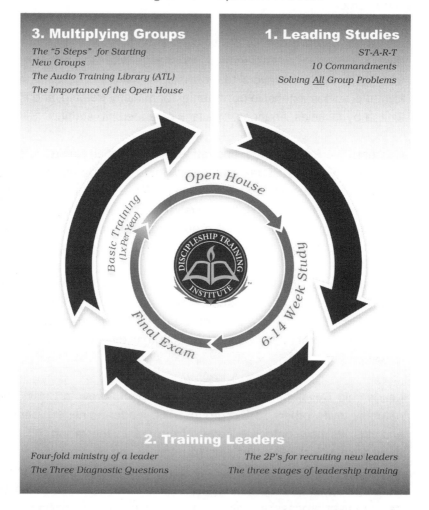

Intentional Discipleship
Training & Development Process

3. Multiplying Groups
The "5 Steps" for Starting New Groups
The Audio Training Library (ATL)
The Importance of the Open House

1. Leading Studies
ST-A-R-T
10 Commandments
Solving All Group Problems

Open House

Basic Training (1x Per Year)

6-14 Week Study

Final Exam

DISCIPLESHIP TRAINING INSTITUTE

2. Training Leaders
Four-fold ministry of a leader
The Three Diagnostic Questions
The 2P's for recruiting new leaders
The three stages of leadership training

How Can I Be Trained?

Included within this Bible study is the student workbook for Level 1 (Basic Training). Level 1 training is both free and optional. Level 1 training teaches you a simple 4-step process (ST-A-R-T) to help you prepare a life-changing Bible study and 10 proven small group leadership principles that will help your group thrive. To register for a Level 1 online training event, either as an individual or as a small group, go to www.LamplightersUSA.org/training or www.discipleUSA.org. If you have additional questions, you can also call 800-507-9516.

INTRODUCTION

Some people believe Ecclesiastes is one of the most puzzling and perplexing books in the Bible, but it answers some of the most profound questions about the meaning of life when it is properly understood. The interpretive "riddle" of Ecclesiastes is easily solved when the book's unique perspective is understood. G. S. Hendry expressed the perspective of the writer of Ecclesiastes well when he stated:

"The writer [of Ecclesiastes] is addressing the general public whose view [of life] is bounded by the horizons of this world; he meets them on their own ground and proceeds to convict them of its inherent vanity. His book is in fact a critique of secularism and secularized religion."

Ecclesiastes was written to help readers realize that life without God leads only to vanity and emptiness. The writer presents several personal examples of trying to find meaning and happiness apart from God and draws conclusions from his observations.

Ecclesiastes also helps believers enter vicariously into the empty lives of the unsaved, their shallow pursuits, their broken dreams, their frustrations, and their confusion. The believer's heart, often cold and critical toward the unsaved, is warmed to overflowing with a spontaneous compassion for the lost.

Ecclesiastes doesn't present the gospel, but the book leads its readers to an obvious question, "How can I know God so I can escape the emptiness of this life?" The answer to this question is found in John's gospel when Jesus said, **"I am the way, the truth, and the life"** (John 14:6; 17:3).

Author and Setting

Ecclesiastes does not identify a human author, but internal evidence within the book points strongly to Solomon, the third king of Israel. The author identified himself as the "son of David," the "king of Israel" (Ecclesiastes 1:1, 12), and one who was wise and possessed great wealth (Ecclesiastes 1:16; 2:7–9). Solomon fits this description well.

The title of the book comes from the word for *preacher* (New International Version [NIV], "Teacher") found in Ecclesiastes 1:1–2, 12. The Hebrew word (*qoheleth*—a speaker of an assembly, leader of an assembly) comes from the Hebrew root *qahal,* which means "to call an assembly." In the Greek version of the Old Testament (known as the Septuagint or LXX), the Hebrew word *qoheleth* is translated "Ecclesiastes." In ancient Greek an ecclesiastes was a wise teacher who addressed an *ecclesia* or assembly of people. The Greek word *ecclesia* is translated "church" in the New Testament.

The wise teacher presents life from the perspective of one who knows God as Creator but not as the Redeemer-Savior. The name *Lord* (*Jehovah*, Redeemer/Savior) does not appear in the book, but the name *Elohim* (the name used of God when referring to creation [Genesis.1:1]) is used regularly throughout the book.

Under the Sun

The repetition of three key words and phrases helps us understand the writer's perspective and enables us to interpret the book correctly. The word *wisdom* (Heb. *hokmah, hokam*) is used twenty-eight times, "under the sun" is used thirty-four times, and "vanity" is used thirty-four times.

The phrase "under the sun" is used frequently throughout the book to remind the reader that the writer is viewing the world from a human perspective—one devoid of an eternal perspective. The wise teacher regularly speaks from a human viewpoint ("under the sun") and then draws conclusions from that perspective. In addition, he offers conclusions about life as it is viewed from "under the sun" and concludes that life without God leads only to vanity and emptiness.

Wisdom Literature

The Old Testament is composed of four different types of literary forms: historical narrative (Genesis through Esther), poetry (Proverbs, Psalms, Song of Solomon), prophecy (Isaiah through Malachi), and wisdom literature (Proverbs, Job, Ecclesiastes). Each type of biblical literature has unique and distinguishable characteristics.

Wisdom literature addresses the practical aspect of life more than any other portion of God's Word. Wisdom literature also makes frequent use of questions, without providing immediate and obvious answers. Finally, wisdom literature addresses some of man's most complex questions: *What is the meaning of life? Why do bad things happen to "good" people? How can I be happy? Why does evil appear to be rewarded?* These questions are not answered immediately in the context, but they are answered in the books known as wisdom literature.

ONE

LIFE IS MEANINGLESS

Read Ecclesiastes 1; other references as given.

Beginning in the fifth century BC, Greek philosophers (Socrates, Plato, Aristotle, and others) sought to understand the meaning of life. In the past twenty-six centuries, secular philosophers have produced various theories about the origin and meaning of life, but none have provided a conclusive answer. Stephen Hawking (1942–2018), the British physicist who was considered the greatest mind since Albert Einstein said, "Scientists will continue to climb the mountain of human understanding until they reach the peak. When they finally reach the apex and look over the other side, they will see that theologians have been there for centuries."

The world's philosophers have asked the right questions, but only God's Word provides the right answer. The Bible says God has **given to us all things that pertain to life and godliness**, including an understanding of who God is and the meaning of life (2 Peter 1:3). God, however, doesn't reveal the secrets of wisdom to the proud or the spiritually lazy (Psalm 10:4; Proverbs 2:1–10). We must be obedient to God's Word and be diligent in our pursuit of wisdom to be the recipients of His truth (John 14:21; Proverbs 2:1-10).

In this first lesson the writer says that life (apart from God) is meaningless. The book of Ecclesiastes then proceeds to take its readers on a journey to discover the meaning of life. In the process, every worldly philosophy is exposed as empty and

Lombardi Time Rule:

If the leader arrives early, he or she has time to pray, prepare the room, and greet others personally.

———

ADD GROUP INSIGHTS BELOW

vain. Before you begin this lesson and each lesson in this study, ask God to reveal Himself to you through His inspired Word.

1. From what perspective is the wise teacher approaching the question of the meaning and purpose of life (Introduction)?

   _____

   _____

   _____

   _____

2. a. Understanding the background and the writer's perspective is essential to understanding Ecclesiastes. What is the meaning of the teacher's use of the important phrase **under the sun** (Introduction)?

   _____

   _____

   b. Give three characteristics of wisdom literature (Introduction).

   1. _____

      _____

   2. _____

      _____

   3. _____

      _____

3. a. How can Ecclesiastes help an unsaved person (Introduction)?

   _____

   b. How can the study of the book of Ecclesiastes help believers (Introduction)?

   _____

_____

_____

_____

Zip-It Rule:

Group members should agree to disagree, but should never be disagreeable.

———

ADDITIONAL INSIGHTS

4. In Ecclesiastes 1:1 Solomon identifies himself primarily as the teacher or preacher (NIV, "teacher"). The specific use of this word (Hebrew, *qoheleth*) in the context indicates he is introducing himself in the formal capacity as one who makes an official address or presents a teaching lecture. Rather than beginning with an introduction to his topic, he begins with a strong assertion (Ecclesiastes 1:2).

   a. What is the meaning of the phrase, **Vanity of vanities, all is vanity** (Ecclesiastes 1:2; NIV, "meaningless")?

   _____

   _____

   b. What *do you think* is the answer to the question the wise teacher asks in Ecclesiastes 1:3?

   _____

   _____

   _____

5. Ecclesiastes is an important part of our inspired Bible (2 Timothy 3:16–17; 2 Peter 1:20–21). Certain passages in the book, however, appear to contradict other portions of God's Word.

   a. How can the wise teacher say that the earth remains forever when the Bible emphatically teaches that the world will be destroyed (Ecclesiastes 1:4; 2 Peter 3:10; Revelation 21:1)?

   _____

   _____

b. Several evidences within Ecclesiastes indicate Solomon assumed the perspective of a natural man—one who possessed an earthly perspective—to prove that life without God is vanity (Ecclesiastes 1:4–11). List four evidences that the wise teacher wrote from man's earthly perspective (life under the sun), rather than God's perspective (Ecclesiastes 1:4–11).

1. _____

_____ (v._____)

2. _____

_____ (v._____)

3. _____

_____ (v._____)

4. _____

_____ (v._____)

6. a. What two things does the Bible teach about the natural man's ability, or inability, to comprehend God and eternity (1 Corinthians 2:14)?

1. _____

2. _____

b. It is difficult for many Christians to focus their affections on the things of God. Even though they know the world is passing away, they still lust after temporal things. Take a moment to honestly examine your life. Do you live **under the sun**? ❏ Yes ❏ No

If you answered Yes, what is it that keeps you so bound to this world in your thinking and desires?

_____

_____

7. Beginning in Ecclesiastes 1:12 Solomon recounts his own experiences of trying to find meaning and happiness in life without God.

   a. In the Bible the word *wisdom* denotes either (1) the fallible reasoning of fallen man or (2) the infallible wisdom of an infinite God (1 Corinthians 1:20–25; James 3:13–18). *Do you think* Solomon was searching for God's wisdom or human wisdom in Ecclesiastes 1:12–17?

   _____

   Why? _____

   _____

   _____

   b. List three things the Bible says about human, or earthly wisdom (1 Corinthians 1:20–25, **the wisdom of this world**).

   1. _____

      _____ (v._____)

   2. _____

      _____ (v._____)

   3. _____

      _____ (v._____)

8. a. The wise teacher said increased (earthly) wisdom and knowledge leads to increased grief and pain (Ecclesiastes 1:18). Why *do you think* this is so?

   _____

   _____

   _____

   _____

Online Training:

Do you want to learn how to disciple another person, become a more effective Bible study leader, or start a new study?? Go to www. LamplightersUSA. org/training to learn how.

———

ADDITIONAL INSIGHTS

   b. What kind of pain, physical or mental/emotional, *do you
       think* he was referring to in Ecclesiastes 1:18?

       _____

9. It's been said that man has only two problems: he doesn't
    know who God is, and he doesn't know who he is in
    relationship to God. When a person does not understand
    God, he cannot comprehend the true meaning of life. What
    must happen before an individual can personally know God
    and comprehend the things of God (John 3:1–8)?

    _____

    _____

    If you are not sure what it means to be born again, turn to
    the back of this study guide and read the Final Exam. It will
    explain how to be born again.

10. What is the most important truth you learned from
    Ecclesiastes chapter 1?

    _____

    _____

    _____

    _____

Two

Pleasure Doesn't Satisfy

Read Ecclesiastes 2; other references as given.

In Ecclesiastes 1, Solomon introduced himself in the official capacity as a wise teacher or sage (Ecclesiastes 1:1), made a bold statement about the emptiness of life (verse 2), supported his claim by reviewing the endless cycles of life (verses 3–11), and offered a personal testimony about his own futile attempts to find meaning in life (verses 12–18). He concluded his quest by saying that there is nothing new under the sun (Ecclesiastes 1:10) and that increased (human) wisdom leads to increased sorrow (verse 18).

In Ecclesiastes chapter 2 Solomon shares his personal testimony (Ecclesiastes 2:1–10) and then draws some important conclusions about life (verses 11–26). Before you begin, ask God to reveal Himself to you and to transform you into the image of His Son.

Volunteer Rule:

If the leader asks for volunteers to read, pray, and answer the questions, group members will be more inclined to invite newcomers.

———

ADD GROUP
INSIGHTS BELOW

1. Where did Solomon turn next in his quest to find meaning in life, and what was his conclusion (Ecclesiastes 2:1–2)?

   _____

2. The wise teacher dedicated eight verses to a discussion of the merits of earthly wisdom (Ecclesiastes 1:13–18), but only two verses to the pursuit of pleasure as a means of fulfillment in life. No thoughtful person has ever seriously believed the pursuit of carnal pleasures brings lasting satisfaction. Jesus

told the story of a prodigal son who pursued unbridled pleasure in his quest for happiness (Luke 15:11–32). The word *prodigal* means "squanderer," and the son wasted his relationship with his family, his reputation, and his earthly inheritance. From his initial rebellion to his return to his father, the prodigal passed through five distinct stages. The five verses listed below identify the five stages. Write a single word or short phrase summarizing each of the five stages of degradation and return. The first one is done for you.

a. Luke 15:12 <u>Rebellion (separation from accountability)</u>

b. Luke 15:13 _____

c. Luke 15:14–16 _____

d. Luke 15:17 _____

e. Luke 15:18 _____

3. a. What was the third thing Solomon pursued in his attempt to find meaning in life (Ecclesiastes 2:4–10)?

   _____

   b. What three things does Solomon (the wise teacher) say about his third attempt to find meaning and fulfillment (Ecclesiastes 2:11)?

   1._____

   _____

   2._____

   _____

   3._____

   _____

4. a. Two words are used in Ecclesiastes 2:1–11 that reveal why Solomon experienced so much dissatisfaction during this period of his life. What are they?

   _____   _____

b. Ecclesiastes 2:1–11 and Romans 7:14–24 are strikingly similar in one point. In Ecclesiastes chapter 2, Solomon is frustrated because his diligent efforts did not bring lasting satisfaction. In Romans chapter 7, Paul testifies that his diligent efforts did not bring victory over sin. What word, used repeatedly in Ecclesiastes 2:1-11 and Romans 7:14–24, provides the reason why most people experience vanity and emptiness in life?

_____

c. When we live from an earthly perspective (**under the sun**), our lives are often characterized by disharmony, discontent, and disunity. In which of the following areas of your thoughts and decision-making is "self" more dominant than God? Circle your answers.

Relationships/marriage   Finances   Prayer

Morality   Work/career   Fashion/Dress

Worship   Entertainment   Health/Diet

Emotions   Speech   Leisure

5. a. The wise teacher drew several conclusions about wisdom and his search for happiness apart from God (Ecclesiastes 2:13–15). What three conclusions did he come to when he compared wisdom and folly (Ecclesiastes 2:13–15)?

1._____

_____ (v. _____)

2._____

_____ (v._____)

3._____

_____ (v._____)

b. What was the wise teacher's summary conclusion about life **under the sun** (Ecclesiastes 2:17)?

59:59 Rule:

Participants appreciate when the leader starts and finishes the studies on time—all in one hour (the 59:59 rule). If the leader doesn't complete the entire lesson, the participants will be less likely to do their weekly lessons and the Bible study discussion will tend to wander.

_____

ADDITIONAL INSIGHTS

_____

_____

_____

c. Have you experienced a time of "emptiness" in your life because you pursued your own worldly dreams rather than God's plan?

❏ Yes   ❏ No   ❏ I don't know if I did.

   If so, when and how did you realize that pursuing your worldly goals wouldn't bring lasting peace and happiness?

_____

_____

6. The wise teacher repeatedly used the phrase **grasping for the wind** (NIV, "chasing after wind"; Ecclesiastes 2:17; 1:14, 17; 2:11). Why do you think this specific word picture appropriately describes man's vain attempts to find peace and satisfaction apart from God?

_____

_____

_____

7. The wise teacher said the pursuit of human wisdom, folly, and self-centered personal achievement led him to hate life (Ecclesiastes 2:17). Next, he analyzed his pursuit of economic achievement as a means of finding happiness and fulfillment (Ecclesiastes 2:18–23).

a. What conclusions did the wise teacher make when he assessed his pursuit of personal and business success apart from God (Ecclesiastes 2:18–23)?

_____

_____

_____

b. Many people who've made financial wealth or career advancement their entire lifetime goal have experienced great problems in their personal lives. What precautions have you taken to ensure that you (and your family) do not fall into the trap that money and (worldly) success buy happiness?

_____

_____

_____

35% Rule:

If the leader talks more than 35% of the time, the group members will be less likely to participate.

———

ADDITIONAL
INSIGHTS

8. Ecclesiastes 2:24–26 forms the first major refrain, or summary statement, in the book. List three conclusions the wise teacher offers at this point in the book (Ecclesiastes 2:24–26).

1. _____

_____ (v._____)

2. _____

_____ (v._____)

3. _____

_____ (v._____)

9. What is the most important truth you learned from Ecclesiastes chapter 2?

_____

_____

_____

_____

ADDITIONAL INSIGHTS

THREE

A TIME FOR EVERYTHING

Read Ecclesiastes 3;
other references as given.

When viewed from an earthly perspective (**under the sun**), life is marked by a lack of peace and joy because we don't understand the meaning of life (Ecclesiastes 1:16–18). If a man focuses on pleasure, his life will be empty (Ecclesiastes 2:1–2). If he focuses on career and business success, his work could suffer an irreversible misfortune, or his success could be lost by those who come after him (Ecclesiastes 2:18–19).

In the first two chapters, the wise teacher quietly introduced a new phrase (**under heaven,** Ecclesiastes 1:13; 2:3). Beginning in chapter 3, he boldly informs his students that God, not man, is the center of life and the source of lasting happiness. Before you begin, ask God to reveal Himself to you and to transform you into the image of His Son.

Focus Rule:

If the leader helps the group members focus on the Bible, they will gain confidence to study God's Word on their own.

ADD GROUP INSIGHTS BELOW

1. Ecclesiastes 3:2–8 serves as an elaboration or explanation of Ecclesiastes 3:1 and as a bridge between two similar passages (Ecclesiastes 2:24–26; 3:12–13). The fourteen comparisons demonstrate that life has endless cycles, but God exercises sovereign control over life. Do you think the events described in Ecclesiastes 3:2–8 are preordained by God regardless of man's involvement, are they simple realities of life which God oversees, or are they something else? Why?

2. The phrases **a time to die** and **a time for war** (Ecclesiastes 3:2, 8) hint at the topics of just wars, capital punishment, and the ongoing "right to die" debate. The concept of a just war has been discussed for hundreds of years, but that debate has escalated due to increased international terrorism.

   a. Imperialism is the policy and practice of one nation attempting to extend its power and dominion over another nation by direct acquisition or by political or economic domination. Pacifism is the attitude or policy of nonresistance, based on the belief that disputes can be settled by nonviolent means. Although some religious sects believe in pacifism, most Christians subscribe to some form of the "just war" concept. In your opinion, when, if any, is a nation's military action justifiable?

   _____

   Why? _____

   _____

   _____

   _____

   _____

   b. What does the Bible teach about capital punishment and the need for the swift execution of justice (Genesis 9:6; Ecclesiastes 8:11; Acts 25:11; Romans 13:4)?

   _____

   _____

   _____

3. A living will is a legal document in which an individual preauthorizes the performance or nonperformance of certain medical procedures (for example, sustained life support, etc.) before a critical health situation occurs.

a. Do you think the advancement of certain life-sustaining medical technology allows man to "play God" by interfering with **a time to die** (Ecclesiastes 3:2), or is the advancement of medicine as it relates to the terminally ill a gift from God? Explain your answer.

_____

_____

_____

_____

If the leader asks all the study questions, the group discussion will be more likely to stay on track.

ADDITIONAL
INSIGHTS

b. Do you think physician-assisted euthanasia (a lethal injection) at the request of a terminally ill patient or the patient's family is right or wrong (Exodus 20:13)?

_____

Why? _____

_____

_____

c. Do you think a Christian is wrong if he or she doesn't authorize the implementation or continuation of certain *extraordinary* medical procedures to sustain the life of a terminally ill patient? (Extraordinary medical procedures are defined as those procedures, such as the continuing use of a respirator, a kidney dialysis machine, or a heart pump, that keep a patient alive.)

_____

_____

_____

4. **A time to embrace, and a time to refrain from embracing** (Ecclesiastes 3:5) may include what's appropriate and inappropriate for believers regarding sexual conduct with other people. Sexual sin in the lives of Christians has brought great reproach on Jesus's name, severe damage to the

testimony of the church, and guilt and brokenness into the lives and marriages of God's people. What is God's will for all Christians regarding sexual conduct (Matthew 5:28; Romans 1:26–27; 1 Corinthians 5:11; 6:18; 1 Thessalonians 4:3)?

_____

_____

_____

5. In ancient Israel people tore their garments at times of severe grief (Genesis 37:29; Joshua. 7:5–6). If **a time to tear** refers to an appropriate time or period to express grief (Ecclesiastes 3:7), what do you think is meant by the phrase **a time to sew** (Ecclesiastes 3:7)?

_____

_____

_____

6. In Ecclesiastes 3:9 the wise teacher asks again if there is any human benefit to living apart from God. Although he previously stated that God is the sole giver of joy (Ecclesiastes 2:24–26), he now questions whether anyone can find lasting fulfillment in their work (Ecclesiastes 3:9). How would you describe the wise teacher's perspective on life at this time (Ecclesiastes 3:9–13)?

_____

_____

_____

7. Benjamin Franklin, a famous American inventor and statesman, once said, "I have lived, sir, a long time, and the longer I live, the more convincing proofs I see of this truth— that God governs in the affairs of men." It is only when we acknowledge God's sovereign control over all aspects of life that we're able to respond to His plan for our lives with joy. Embracing God's sovereignty keeps us from becoming

frustrated with the problems and trials we cannot control (Ecclesiastes 3:2–8).

a.   What gift has God given all people to help them see life from His perspective (Ecclesiastes 3:11)?

_____

_____

b.   The fact that God has set eternity in every man's heart has profound implications on the subject of evangelism. In what ways do you think this great spiritual truth should affect a Christian's efforts and methods of reaching the lost?

_____

_____

_____

8.   God has arranged this world so that nothing can be changed or altered by man (Ecclesiastes 3:14). Interestingly, many insurance companies unwittingly acknowledge God's sovereignty when their policies contain clauses that exclude "acts of God" such as floods and tornados.

a.   What is God's motivation for arranging the affairs of life (Ecclesiastes 3:14; Ephesians 1:10)?

_____

_____

b.   What spiritual lessons do you think a Christian should learn from the knowledge of God's sovereign control over the affairs of life (Romans 8:28, 1 Thessalonians 5:18)?

_____

_____

_____

Has your group become a "Holy huddle?" Learn how to reach out to others by taking online leadership training.

ADDITIONAL INSIGHTS

9. In Ecclesiastes 3:16, the wise teacher saw two unfortunate situations, **In the place of judgment, wickedness was there**, and **in the place of righteousness, iniquity was there**. Without mentioning specific names, give at least two examples of wickedness or iniquity found in places of justice and righteousness.

    _____

    _____

    _____

    _____

10. God guides the affairs of life to show us our limitations and teach us to fear Him (Ecclesiastes 3:14). God also tests men (Ecclesiastes 3:18). What do you think is meant by the statement **that they may see that they themselves are like animals** (Ecclesiastes 3:18)?

    _____

    _____

11. a. The wise teacher said the fate of men and beasts is the same, and there is no advantage for men over beasts (Ecclesiastes 3:19–20). Since all men will be judged after they die (2 Corinthians 5:10; Hebrews 9:27; Revelation 20:11–15), what do you think these verses mean?

    _____

    _____

    b. What conclusions about life did the wise teacher present to his listeners who viewed life from the perspective of **under the sun** (Ecclesiastes 3:22)?

    _____

    _____

    _____

Four

The Sacrifice of Fools

Read Ecclesiastes 4–5; other references as given.

In the previous lesson you learned that God controls the endless cycles in life (Ecclesiastes 3:2–8). You also learned that God places eternity in the hearts of all men (Ecclesiastes 3:11). He also sets limits on man's ability to accomplish his goals to help him come to his senses and glorify God rather than himself (Ecclesiastes 3:14). Man finds the joy and peace he longs for when he is fully surrendered to God.

In Ecclesiastes chapter 4, the wise teacher addresses oppression (Ecclesiastes 4:1–3), envy (verses 5–6), companionship (verses 7–12), and the unfortunate legacy of foolish conduct (verses 13–16). In chapter 5, he addresses the importance of reverence for God and the importance of having a right perspective on work. Before you begin this lesson, ask God to reveal Himself and to transform you into the image of His Son.

Gospel Gold Rule:

Try to get all the answers to the questions—not just the easy ones. Go for the gold.

ADD GROUP
INSIGHTS BELOW

1. Any legitimate discussion about life and God must eventually address the subject of injustice. Both Christians and non-Christians struggle with the concept of a just Creator and what appears to be an unjust creation. To nonbelievers, injustice proves one of three things: (1) God is not sovereign, (2) God is not good, or (3) God does not exist. When believers see injustice, they (1) question God's love ("Does God really love me?"), (2) question God's sovereignty ("Is God really in control?"), or (3) trust God to work what is.

a. What does the wise teacher say about oppression in this world (Ecclesiastes 4:1–3)?

_____

_____

b. What was his reaction to all the evil and oppression he saw (Ecclesiastes 4:2–3)?

_____

_____

2. a. In Ecclesiastes 4:4–12 the wise teacher returns to the question of whether labor done **under the sun** (that is, work strictly for man's benefit) has any lasting value. What is one of man's primary motivations for economic advancement (Ecclesiastes 4:4)?

_____

b. Healthy competition among individual workers and rival companies has led to world-changing innovations and increased productivity. Unbridled rivalry, however, can lead to destruction, imprisonment, and even death when winning becomes everything. What is another sinful response to work (Ecclesiastes 4:5)?

_____

3. The wise teacher used an illustration of a man who was diligent in his labor but had no heir. He was too preoccupied with his work to consider some important things in life. What were they (Ecclesiastes 4:8)?

_____

_____

4. List four benefits a person receives when he or she works with other people (Ecclesiastes 4:9–12).

1. _____
   _____ (v. ___)

2. _____
   _____ (v. ___)

3. _____
   _____ (v. ___)

4. _____
   _____ (v. ___)

Want to learn how to disciple another person, lead a life-changing Bible study or start another study? Go to www.Lamplighters USA.org/training to learn how.

―――――

ADDITIONAL INSIGHTS

5. a. In the illustration of the old king and the poor youth, why was the poor wise lad better than the old foolish king (Ecclesiastes 4:13)?

   _____
   _____

   b. What negative human characteristics did the foolish king and his subjects exhibit (Ecclesiastes 4:14–16)?

   _____
   _____

6. True satisfaction in life comes from embracing God's plan and rejoicing in His gifts, not from living a self-centered life devoid of an eternal perspective. Even though man is unable to fully comprehend the eternal dimension, he should seek to understand God's ways.

   a. True worship is God's means of moving man from being self-centered to being God-focused. What two commands are given regarding public worship (Ecclesiastes 5:1)?

      1. _____
         _____

      2. _____
         _____

b. The wise teacher used some powerful language to describe insincere worship. What do you think is meant by the phrase **the sacrifice of fools** (Ecclesiastes 5:1; see also Jeremiah 7:1–11; Mark 5:5–9)?

_____

_____

7. The Hebrew word for **walk prudently** (*shamar*) means "to keep, guard, observe, or protect." What do you think it means to **walk prudently when you go to the house of God** (Ecclesiastes 5:1)?

_____

_____

_____

8. Ecclesiastes 5:1–7 gives nine commands regarding the proper worship of God. Each of these commands can be personalized to form an action step (example, **Walk prudently when you go to the house of God**—*I should prepare myself before I worship God*). Personalize four of the remaining eight commands, making each one a personal action step for more effective public worship (Ecclesiastes 5:1–7; remember to start every personalized action step with the words *I should* or *I will*). The first one is done for you as an example.

a. Ecclesiastes 5:2: <u>I will quiet my heart and limit my speech and others as I prepare to worship.</u>

b. Ecclesiastes 5:4: _____

_____

c. Ecclesiastes 5:6: _____

_____

d. Ecclesiastes 5:7: _____

_____

9. During the Old Testament period, God designated two places for the Israelites to worship. The tabernacle was a tent-like worship center the Israelites transported during their forty years of wilderness wanderings (Exodus 40:36–40). The temple was a permanent structure built by Solomon in Jerusalem on the very location where Abraham offered his son Isaac (Genesis. 22:1–14). Presently, the Islamic Dome of the Rock, or the Mosque of Omar, stands on this site. Many Christians are confused about the location of God's temple in the New Testament period. Where, if anywhere, is the earthly temple of God located during the New Testament period (1 Corinthians 6:19–20)?

_____

_____

10. The Bible gives some strong words of exhortation regarding the making and keeping of vows (Ecclesiastes 5:5, **Better not to vow than to vow and not pay**). Do you think it's wrong for a Christian to make a vow (Matthew 5:33–37; James 5:12)? Why? _____

_____

_____

_____

11. In Ecclesiastes 5:8–17 Solomon returned to his original theme that life from man's perspective is empty. He addressed the oppression of the poor and other forms of political corruption. One of the responsibilities of government is to make righteous laws and execute justice on lawbreakers (Romans 13:3). When the citizens of a nation observe political corruption, they often become discouraged with both government and the lawmakers. How should believers respond to both social and political injustice (Ecclesiastes 5:8)? Why?

_____

_____

_____

Did you know Lamplighters is more than a small group ministry? It is a discipleship training ministry that uses a small group format to train disciple-makers. If every group trained one person per study, God would use these new disciple-makers to reach more people for Christ.

———

ADDITIONAL INSIGHTS

_____

_____

12. a. What are some problems faced by those who love money or the things money can buy (Ecclesiastes 5:10–11; 1 Timothy 6:9)?

_____

_____

_____

b. **The abundance of the rich will not permit him to sleep** (Ecclesiastes 5:12). List three reasons why you think an individual who loves money does not find peace and satisfaction in life .

1. _____

_____

2. _____

_____

3. _____

_____

13. During man's brief life he will observe social injustice (Ecclesiastes 5:8), vanity (Ecclesiastes 5:10), and misfortune (Ecclesiastes 5:16, **severe evil**; NIV, "grievous evil"). Life does, however, offer some consolation. Ecclesiastes 5:18–20 forms the third return to this point in the book (Ecclesiastes 2:24–26, 3:22). In this summary statement the wise teacher draws some conclusions about life from man's perspective. Where can all men find some degree of pleasure in this life (Ecclesiastes 5:18–20)?

_____

_____

_____

FIVE

WORK DOESN'T SATISFY

Read Ecclesiastes 6; other references as given.

God promises abundant joy to those who submit to His will and walk in His ways (John 15:10–11). To experience this joy, you must view life from God's perspective (Ecclesiastes 1:2–2:26), submit daily to His sovereign plan (Ecclesiastes 3:14), and rejoice in whatever He provides. You must also remember that God allows injustice and wickedness to exist in this world as He works out His sovereign plan.

Many believers fail to experience joy because they view life from man's perspective (**under the sun**) rather than from an eternal perspective. In this lesson the Bible identifies several situations in life that don't make sense when life is viewed **under the sun**. Now before you begin, humble yourself before God and ask Him to reveal Himself to you through His inspired Word.

No-Trespassing Rule:

To keep the Bible study on track, avoid talking about political parties, church denominations, and Bible translations.

ADD GROUP INSIGHTS BELOW

1. a. Ecclesiastes 6:1–2 presents a hypothetical situation in life (**common among men**) that he describes as **an evil affliction** (NIV, "grievous evil"). The Hebrew word (*choliy ra*) means "evil sickness" or "malignant disease" and refers to something particularly distressing. What was it (Ecclesiastes 6:1–2)?

    _____

    _____

    _____

b. Give at least two examples of how this might happen.

1. _____

_____

2. _____

_____

2. The Bible reminds us that God's blessings don't guarantee man's happiness or satisfaction (Ecclesiastes 6:3). Under the Old Testament law, children were considered a tangible expression of God's blessing and barrenness was considered a curse (Genesis 30:1–2; Deuteronomy 28:4, 11, 18). Material prosperity and divine protection from enemies were also considered evidence of God's blessings upon His people (Deuteronomy 28:8, 10, 12).

a. The teacher described a man who apparently received God's blessings (Ecclesiastes 6:3, **If a man begets a hundred children and lives many years**). What two things happened to the individual that caused the wise teacher to say **a stillborn child is better than he** (Ecclesiastes 6:3–4)?

1. _____

_____

2. _____

_____

b. The Bible teaches that life without God is futile (Ecclesiastes 2:1, 17). Do you think the word *it* refers to this man's life or the miscarriage in Ecclesiastes 6:3–5?

_____

Why? _____

_____

_____

3. The Bible is clear in its teaching that God is the sole giver of joy in life. He also said that no one could take this joy from them (John 16:24). Jesus told His disciples, **"These things I have spoken to you, that My joy may remain in you, and that your joy may be full"** (John 15:11).

   a. Upon what single condition or prerequisite can believers experience this divine joy that can never be taken from them?

   _____

   b. Other than an abiding relationship with Jesus Christ, where do you think people look for genuine joy and true happiness in life?

   _____

   _____

   _____

   c. Where do you look for joy and peace in your life?

   _____

   _____

   _____

4. Every person experiences trials in life (Job 5:7; 14:1). Some people believe their problems are more difficult by others and Satan uses our dissatisfaction with our circumstances to rob our joy and trap us into envying other people. In Psalm 73 the psalmist Asaph recounted his own jealousy when he reflected on the apparent successes of the wicked from a human perspective.

   a. Asaph made several faulty conclusions when he considered the successes of those he thought more fortunate. Please name at least four (Psalm 73:2–16).

      1. _____

      _____

If you use table tents or name tags, it will help visitors feel more comfortable and new members will be assimilated more easily into your group.

ADDITIONAL INSIGHTS

2. _____

_____

3. _____

_____

4. _____

_____

b. When Asaph stopped looking at the apparent success of others from man's perspective (**under the sun**), his entire outlook changed. Rather than being envious, discouraged, and frustrated, he became grateful and compassionate. What caused his perspective to change so drastically (Psalm 73:17–28)?

_____

_____

_____

5. Whether a family has one or a hundred children, they are all a gift and blessing from God (Psalm 127:3). While some Christian couples believe they should raise as many children as God gives them, others wonder if using some form of birth control is right or wrong. What advice would you give a Christian friend seeking counsel regarding "family planning"?

_____

_____

_____

_____

6. The teacher identified two universal realities that led him to question whether a wise man has any advantage over the fool. What are they (Ecclesiastes 6:6–8)?

1. _____

Use the side margins to write down spiritual insights from other people in your group. Add the person's name and the date to help you remember in the future.

ADDITIONAL INSIGHTS

2. _____

7. If a man strives to fulfill his own desires, his soul will never be satisfied (Ecclesiastes 6:7). You know that living **under the sun** leads to an empty life. Hopefully, you also realize your need to understand God's will for your life. Using what you've learned so far from your study of Ecclesiastes, develop an abbreviated personal action plan for each of the following areas of your life.

Worship (personal and corporate): _____

_____

_____

Career/work: _____

_____

_____

Finances and talents: _____

_____

_____

8. The teacher described people who have pursued their life goals, but they have not found lasting satisfaction. How do you think a believer can know for certain if the things he is pursuing in life will bring lasting fulfillment and satisfaction?

_____

_____

_____

_____

9. God has established unchangeable laws for man to live by and communicated these laws in His Word. They cannot

change because His Word is unchangeable (Psalm 119:89; John 10:35).

a. What important truths about God and life does the wise teacher add in Ecclesiastes 6:10–12?

_____

_____

_____

_____

b. God is mightier than man (Ecclesiastes 6:10). How should this important theological truth affect your life?

_____

_____

_____

_____

10. What is the most important truth you learned from this lesson?

_____

_____

_____

_____

_____

_____

Six

True Righteousness

**Read Ecclesiastes 7;
other references as given.**

God is the source and giver of joy. There is no lasting joy or fulfillment in life apart from Him. The uncertainties of life (misfortune, death, oppression, wickedness, etc.) press upon our hearts and threaten to rob us of joy, but the one who knows that God is also working behind the scenes overcomes (1 John 5:4).

In Ecclesiastes chapter 7, the wise teacher continues to instruct us on what doesn't work in life (living **under the sun**). As he did in the first few chapters, he informs his students how to live wisely. Only by acquiring God's wisdom are we able to gain satisfaction in life.

Before you begin, ask God to reveal Himself to you through His inspired Word and transform you into the image of Jesus Christ.

Transformation
Rule:

Seek for personal
transformation,
not mere
information, from
God's Word.

———

ADD GROUP
INSIGHTS BELOW

1. Ecclesiastes 7:1–14 is proverbial, meaning there is a close relationship between the first and second lines of each verse. In Ecclesiastes 7:1, the wise teacher uses a figure of speech called a paronomasia to compare two Hebrew words of similar sound (*shem* meaning "name," and *shemen* meaning "ointment"). What does it mean to have a good name?

_____

_____

2. Why is it better for people to go to a funeral (**the house of mourning**) than a dinner party (**the house of feasting**, Ecclesiastes 7:2)?

_____

_____

3. In Ecclesiastes 7:2–6 the Bible appears to be censoring laughter and happiness, but it is rejecting the senseless merriment that characterizes those who ignore life's realities. The wise teacher uses the phrases **the heart of fools, the song of fools**, and **the laughter of the fool** (Ecclesiastes 7:4–6) to describe those who mask the emptiness of their shallow lives with mirth and folly. Give at least three examples of shallow, worldly pleasures that often keep men and women from pursuing what can truly satisfy.

1. _____

_____

2. _____

_____

3. _____

_____

4. a. Believers should avoid fools because of their negative influence on others (Psalm 1:1, 4–5; 1 Corinthians 15:33). The wise teacher gives several characteristics of fools in the first part of Ecclesiastes chapter 7. Please list at least four (Ecclesiastes 7:4–9).

1. _____

_____

2. _____

_____

3. _____

_____

4. _____

_____

Would you like to learn how to prepare a life-changing Bible study using a simple 4-step process? Contact Lamplighters and ask about ST-A-R-T.

———

ADDITIONAL INSIGHTS

b. The Bible says **anger rests in the bosom of fools** (Ecclesiastes 7:9), indicating that the fool has embraced anger, making it his companion. Just as it's impossible for a Christian to believe in a sovereign God and have a "victim mentality," it's impossible to be a grateful Christian (1 Thessalonians 5:18) and allow anger to be your constant companion. Most anger is either a sinful attempt to control other people, or it stems from a fear related to something for which the believer is unwilling to trust God. Either way, it's an indication that an individual has not fully surrendered a particular area of his life to God. In what specific area(s) of your life have you allowed anger to be your companion? Circle the areas of your life in which you need to stop letting anger be your companion.

Work   Marriage   Family Relations
Driving   Conversation/Listening
Friends and Relatives   Past Hurts/Offences
Finances   Others

c. If you've allowed anger to rest in your heart, are you willing to repent of your sin and trust God in this area of your life?

_____

d. Is there someone from whom you need to seek forgiveness for your anger towards them in the past?

_____

5. List two things the Bible says about times of prosperity and adversity (Ecclesiastes 7:14).

1. _____

_____

2. _____

_____

6. The wise teacher observed more realities of life that can't be fully understood from a human perspective (Ecclesiastes 7:15–29). What new observations did he make that led him to believe that life from an earthly perspective was valueless (Ecclesiastes 7:15)?

_____

_____

_____

7. Ecclesiastes 7:16–17 appears to be one of the most obvious contradictions in Scripture. God's people are commanded to be righteous (Philippians 2:12; Titus 2:12), to love God supremely (Luke 10:27), and to sacrifice their lives for God's glory and service (Romans 12:1). Do you think Ecclesiastes 7:16 is simply the assessment of an individual who views life from a natural perspective—one who's unable to see any earthly benefit to righteous living—or is it teaching something altogether different? If so, what?

_____

_____

_____

8. The key to interpreting Ecclesiastes 7:16 correctly is the word **overly** (NIV, "overrighteous"). In the New Testament the Pharisees attempted to be righteous, but they received the scathing rebuke of Jesus (Matthew 23:27–28). In the same way, the Galatian believers received one of the apostle Paul's harshest rebukes for their attempts to be righteous (Galatians 3:1–5).

a. Why do you think some individuals, including believers, adopt a faulty concept of righteousness that leads them to pursue a distorted approach to spiritual growth—one based on self-effort rather than trusting Jesus Christ?

_____

_____

_____

b. A Christian shouldn't practice the wrong type of righteousness, and he should stay away from sin. How can a believer maintain this delicate spiritual balance in his Christian life (Ecclesiastes 7:18)?

_____

_____

_____

9. A careful study of the Scriptures reveals three types of righteousness: (1) positional righteousness—a believer's eternally-forgiven, legal standing before God as a result of his salvation in Christ (2 Corinthians 5:21); (2) practical righteousness—the consistent, godly behavior of a believer, reflecting his heavenly heritage in Christ (Matthew 1:19, a just, upright, or righteous man); and (3) ultimate righteousness, or glorification—the spiritual transformation that takes place in a believer when he stands in the presence of Jesus Christ for the first time (1 John 3:1–2). Which of the three types of righteousness is referred to in Ecclesiastes 7:16?
   1. Positional Righteousness
   2. Practical Righteousness
   3. Ultimate Righteousness

10. The wise teacher offers some excellent practical advice about biblical communication. What is it (Ecclesiastes 7:21–22)?

_____

_____

_____

11. a. Solomon was disappointed in his attempts to understand the deep mysteries of life. What two conclusions did he come to (Ecclesiastes 7:23–25)?

1. _____

_____

2. _____

_____

b. If a man truly fears the Lord, his life will be pleasing to God. What other benefit will a believer gain if he allows a healthy fear of the Lord to permeate his life (Ecclesiastes 7:26)?

_____

_____

12 In Ecclesiastes 7:27–28, the wise teacher continued to teach on the depths of wisdom. Speaking from personal experience (Ecclesiastes 7:27, **Here is what I have found**), he could find only one man in a thousand, and not one woman in a thousand, who truly understood wisdom.

a. What do the Scriptures reveal about Solomon's life that led him to such a dismal observation about mankind in general and woman in particular (1 Kings 11:1–3)?

_____

_____

_____

b. The wise teacher said this world is filled with sin (Ecclesiastes 7:20), backbiting (7:21–22), and unrighteous men and women (7:26, 28). If God is the sovereign ruler of this world, why isn't He to blame for all this mess (Ecclesiastes 7:29)?

_____

_____

Seven

Who Is Wise?

Read Ecclesiastes 8; other references as given.

In the book of Proverbs, wisdom is defined as knowledge and understanding (Proverbs 2:6) and it has been said that wisdom is God-given knowledge humbly put to work. To be wise, an individual must (1) know God's truth, (2) understand how to apply God's truth, and (3) obey God's truth in all aspects of life.

In Ecclesiastes 8:1 the teacher asks a question: "Who is like a wise man?" The wise teacher's question is reminiscent of the one James asks, "Who is wise and understanding among you?" (James 3:13). Both questions encourage us to examine how we live in this world. The wise teacher answers his rhetorical question (Who is wise?) by presenting several wise responses to a variety of life circumstances. Now ask God to reveal Himself to you and to transform you into the image of Jesus Christ.

1. a. Although no man can plumb the depths of God's wisdom, you should pursue wisdom because it offers protection (Ecclesiastes 7:12) and **strengthens the wise more than ten rulers** (Ecclesiastes 7:19). What other benefit can an individual gain from acquiring wisdom (Ecclesiastes 8:1)?

_____

_____

Drawing Rule:

To learn how to draw everyone into the group discussion without calling on anyone, go to www.Lamplighters USA.org/training.

ADD GROUP
INSIGHTS BELOW

b. Why do you think wisdom makes an individual's face shine (Ecclesiastes 8:1; NIV, "brighten his face")?

_____

_____

_____

_____

2. a. In Ecclesiastes 8:2 the wise teacher exhorts his readers to obey the governing authorities God has placed over their lives. Circle the following laws that you believe all Christians should obey.

speed/driving laws   zoning laws   tax laws
property laws   voting laws
copyright laws (including music, video, books)
intellectual property laws   immigration laws

b. Do you think there are situations when it is okay to violate any of these laws? _____

Why? _____

_____

_____

3. Throughout history Christians have frequently lived under tyrannical governments. What spiritual truth is taught in both the Old and New Testaments regarding a Christian's duty to human government, including those that are unrighteous (Ecclesiastes 8:2; Romans 13:1–5)?

_____

_____

_____

4. Millions of people, including countless Christians, have been murdered by despotic world leaders. Knowing this to be true, what do you think is meant by the statement **he who**

keeps his [the king's] **command will experience nothing harmful** (Ecclesiastes 8:5)?

_____

_____

_____

5. a. Many despotic leaders have oppressed their people to the point that their subjects rebel. When this happens, believers find themselves in a very difficult situation. What specific counsel does the Bible give believers who find themselves in oppressive political situations (Ecclesiastes 8:3–6)?

_____

_____

   b. What do you think is the meaning of the phrase **for every matter there is a time and judgment** (Ecclesiastes 8:6; NIV, "proper time and procedure")?

_____

_____

   c. The immediate context of Ecclesiastes 8:6 refers to tyrannical government leaders. Many believers, however, work daily under the leadership of unreasonable authorities. Do you think a Christian could apply this same principle if he or she is working in a hostile employment environment?   ❑ Yes   ❑ No

   If you answered "Yes," in what way do you think this principle could apply to the workplace?

_____

_____

_____

_____

6. The believer is cautioned against being hasty to join an insurrection (**there is a time and judgment**, Ecclesiastes 8:6). Why should a believer be cautious about joining a cause, even though at the time it appears just (Ecclesiastes 8:7–8)?

_____

_____

_____

7. Life doesn't make sense without God. In fact, life *cannot* make sense without God. To the unsaved (unregenerate) man, life is empty because there are too many unanswerable questions and inconsistencies. Even for believers, the righteous man often doesn't appear to have any advantages in this life over the wicked man because they both die and enter the grave (Ecclesiastes 6:6). The wise teacher mentions an additional factor about life **under the sun** that adds to the vanity of life. What is it (Ecclesiastes 8:10)?

_____

_____

_____

8. a. What can the righteous (**those who fear God**) expect for their devotion to God (Ecclesiastes 8:12)?

_____

_____

   b. If a person fears God, he will obey God, love others (including his family), and he will serve the Lord joyously and wholeheartedly. What happens if a believer is more concerned about pleasing people than fearing God (Proverbs 29:25; Galatians 1:10)?

_____

_____

9. a. The teacher says there is a righteous man who perishes in his righteousness and a wicked man who prolongs his life in his wickedness (Ecclesiastes 7:15). How can he now say that it will not go well for the evil man, and he will not lengthen his days like a shadow (Ecclesiastes 8:13)?

   _____

   _____

Would you like to learn how to lead someone through this same study? It's not hard. Go to www.Lamplighters USA.org to register for *free* online leadership training.

———

ADDITIONAL INSIGHTS

   b. Sometimes the wicked are blessed and the righteous experience trouble (Ecclesiastes 8:14). Although both the unsaved and the saved see this, they respond differently. The believer continues to serve God, knowing that someday God will judge everything. How does the one who lives from an earthly perspective (**under the sun**) respond to this "injustice" (Ecclesiastes 8:15)?

   _____

   _____

   c. Have you ever felt that life wasn't fair, and the only point of life was to amuse yourself (eat, drink, and be merry)?
   ❏ Yes   ❏ No

   How did you come to realize that life did have meaning and there was more to life than just having a good time?

   _____

   _____

   _____

10. a. Throughout Scripture the repetition of certain words or phrases is used for emphasis and serves as a valuable teaching tool. What phrase is repeated three times in the last verse of this chapter, and what do you think it means (Ecclesiastes 8:17)?

   _____

b. Take a minute to seriously evaluate your life goals and the things you want in your life. Do you honestly believe that the things you are pursuing will give you the satisfaction and fulfillment you are longing for?

_____

_____

Why do you believe it to be true?

_____

_____

_____

11. What is the most important truth you learned in this lesson?

_____

_____

_____

_____

Eight

Time and Chance

**Read Ecclesiastes 9;
other references as given.**

The hedonist believes pleasure is man's highest goal in life. He is busy entertaining himself and never really thinks about the meaning of life. The secularist (atheist, agnostic) is pridefully overconfident in his intellectual abilities and believes man will ultimately discover the deep mysteries of life and the universe. He refuses to acknowledge God in his thoughts, and God withholds the deep mysteries of life from the prideful (Ecclesiastes 3:14, 2 Corinthians 1:14).

In Ecclesiastes chapter 9, the Bible reminds us that time and chance overtake all men. Even wise living does not guarantee a long, healthy life (Ecclesiastes 9:7–9). Now ask God to reveal Himself to you and to transform you into the image of Jesus Christ.

Balance Rule:

To learn how to balance the group discussion, go to www.Lamplighters USA.org/training or call 800 507-9516.

———

ADD GROUP INSIGHTS BELOW

1. The wise teacher continues to draw conclusions from life. His readers are being shown that life without God cannot bring fulfillment. What new conclusions did the wise teacher draw from his assessment of the things he observed (Ecclesiastes 9:1–3)?

    1. _____

    _____ (v. _____)

    2. _____

    _____ (v. _____)

3. _____

_____ (v. _____)

4. _____

_____ (v. _____)

2. a. How does he describe man's spiritual condition (Ecclesiastes 7:20; 9:3)?

_____

_____

b. How did the apostle Paul describe man's spiritual condition in his letter to the Roman believers (Romans 3:10–12)?

_____

_____

c. How did Paul describe the human condition to the Ephesian believers (Ephesians 2:1–3, 12)?

_____

_____

_____

3. Conservative theologians use the term "total depravity" to describe man's spiritual condition before the time of salvation through faith in Jesus Christ. What aspects of man's being have been scarred by the effects of sin (Jeremiah 17:9; Romans 8:10; 2 Corinthians 4:4)?

_____

_____

_____

4. Dogs in ancient Israel were unlike the pedigreed pets found in first-world countries today. They were mangy scavengers,

and to call someone a dog was to speak very disrespectfully of that person (Philippians 3:2). On the other hand, lions were considered noble beasts. The wise teacher said a live dog is better than a dead lion (Ecclesiastes 9:4). What was the point of his comparison (Ecclesiastes 9:4–6)?

_____

_____

_____

5. With all our problems and innate inability to discover the meaning of life, we can easily become despondent and give up on life. However, the wise teacher gave sound practical advice to all who can accept it. What is it (Ecclesiastes 9:7–10)?

_____

_____

6. It may seem strange that the Bible talks about chance until you remember that Ecclesiastes was written from the perspective of **under the sun** (Ecclesiastes 9:9). Non-Christians use the terms "good luck" and "bad luck" to describe the positive and negative things that happen unexpectedly in their lives. Christians understand that these blessings and misfortunes (from a human perspective) are God's unannounced, sovereign acts of intervention in their lives. Victory in the race of life isn't guaranteed to the swift or the strong; provision (**bread**; NIV, "food") isn't guaranteed to the wise; financial wealth isn't guaranteed to those with understanding, and favor isn't guaranteed to people of skill. What do you think should be the motivating factor in a believer's life?

_____

_____

_____

Planning to have an Open House to introduce your next study? Lamplighters offers a brief audio introduction for each study and a helpful Welcome booklet to guide you through the Open House.

ADDITIONAL INSIGHTS

7. The teacher encourages his readers to enjoy the simple pleasures of life, work, and family, even though there is no guarantee of a future, earthly reward. Those who trust in Jesus Christ alone for eternal life, however, have the guarantee of eternal life, which is based upon Christ's finished work on the cross (1 John 5:13).

   a. What two things overtake all men that may prevent them from reaping the benefits of their labor (Ecclesiastes 9:11–12)?

   _____

   _____

   b. Since time and chance overtake every man (Ecclesiastes 9:12, **the sons of men are snared in an evil time, when it falls suddenly upon them**), are you absolutely certain that you are born again?
   ❑ Yes   ❑ No   ❑ I am not completely sure

   If you're not certain, turn to the back of this study guide, and read the Final Exam over carefully. It will explain from the Bible how you can receive the gift of eternal life.

8. Jesus told a parable of a rich businessman who made careful plans for future expansion (Luke 12:16–21). As the businessman prepared, however, he overlooked one critical factor. What was it?

   _____

   _____

9. The Bible teaches that for both the unsaved and the saved, death can come at any time. Some Christians who fail to prepare for an untimely death leave their families in difficult circumstances, both financially and administratively. What physical and practical preparations do you think a Christian should make, if possible, to ensure that remaining family

members don't experience unnecessary hardship because of sudden death?

_____

_____

It's a good time to begin praying and inviting new people for your next Open House.

———————

ADDITIONAL INSIGHTS

10. The wise teacher said that he hated life (Ecclesiastes 2:17), but we should enjoy life (Ecclesiastes 3:12). He said we're not to be overly righteous (Ecclesiastes 7:16–17), but we should fear God (Ecclesiastes 5:7). Should a believer hate life, enjoy life, live for now, or live for eternity? In other words, what do you think is the proper perspective on life for a Christian?

_____

_____

_____

_____

11. Again the wise teacher lauds the value of gaining wisdom. What three things is wisdom better than (Ecclesiastes 9:13–18)?

1. _____

   _____ (v. _____)

2. _____

   _____ (v. _____)

3. _____

   _____ (v. _____)

12. What is the most important spiritual truth you learned from this lesson?

_____

_____

_____

ADDITIONAL INSIGHTS

NINE

RISK AND REWARD

Read Ecclesiastes 10; other references as given.

In the previous lesson you learned that time and chance overtake all men. You also learned that God wants you to love life to the fullest. For many people the term "human existence" is an apt and unfortunate summary of their lives, but for the one who knows God and obeys His will, this brief life should be lived to the fullest. As one famous line from a movie says, "Get busy living, or get busy dying." Ecclesiastes teaches believers to get busy living.

In Ecclesiastes 10, the wise teacher warns his listeners about another danger, a single act of folly. One foolish act can ruin a person's reputation and cause great harm (Ecclesiastes 10:1–10, 18). Since no one is entirely wise, we must guard against committing a foolish act that can destroy much good.

Now before you begin this lesson, humble yourself before God, and ask Him to reveal Himself to you through His inspired Word.

1. What important truth about life is taught in Ecclesiastes 10:1?

    _____

    _____

2. A single act of folly can outweigh a lifetime of wisdom and honorable conduct. Throughout Scripture, many lives

Is your study going well? Consider starting a new group. To learn how, go to www. Lamplighters USA.org/training.

ADD GROUP INSIGHTS BELOW

have been greatly harmed by a single act of folly. From the following references, list the individuals and their act of foolishness that marred their lives and testimonies.

a. Joshua 7:1, 19–21: _____

_____

b. 1 Samuel 15:17–26: _____

_____

c. 2 Samuel 11:1–5; 12:13–14: _____

_____

d. Galatians 2:11–13: _____

_____

3. When Christians learn that some great men and women of faith failed to live a consistently godly life, they are often tempted to be fearful. They believe they might also stumble in their Christian lives, bringing reproach on themselves, their families, and the name of Jesus Christ.

a. What assurance does God give believers about living a consistent Christian life that is free of folly (2 Peter 1:3–11)?

_____

_____

b. What spiritual qualities must be present in a Christian's life before he can be assured of God's promise (2 Peter 1:5–7)?

_____

_____

c. Which, if any, of these spiritual qualities is lacking in your life and might eventually cause you to stumble in your Christian life?

_____

_____

It's time to choose your next study. Turn to the back of the study guide for a list of available studies or go online for the latest studies.

ADDITIONAL INSIGHTS

d. If a believer diligently follows Christ, he can trust God to keep him from stumbling. However, if he is not diligent to allow God to develop these spiritual qualities in himself, he forfeits some very important spiritual benefits. Please name four of them (2 Peter 1:8–9).

1. _____

2. _____

3. _____

4. _____

4. a. The Bible says, **A wise man's heart is at his right hand, but a fool's heart at his left** (Ecclesiastes 10:2). What does the right hand signify in Scripture (Psalm 16:8; 110:5; 121:5)?

_____

b. What does a fool's heart direct towards (Ecclesiastes 10:2)? What do you think this means?

_____

_____

_____

5. When a person in a position of authority loses his or her temper, those in positions of subordination are tempted to react sinfully because they feel attacked and emotionally abused. What advice does God's Word give about how to respond to those who use anger to control or intimidate (Ecclesiastes 10:4)?

_____

_____

6. The wise teacher turned his attention from observing folly in the lives of individuals to observing folly in society in general. What was the wise teacher referring to when he said **There is an evil I have seen under the sun** (Ecclesiastes 10:5–7)?

_____

_____

7. Ecclesiastes 10:8–11 is a single unit that teaches some important lessons about the benefits of wisdom. In these verses, there are four proverbs (Ecclesiastes 10:8–10a, 11) and an important summary statement (Ecclesiastes 10:10, **But wisdom brings success**). Wisdom offers its possessor an advantage, but it doesn't eliminate all risks or problems in life.

   a. List three important lessons about wisdom taught in Ecclesiastes 10:8–11.

   1._____

   _____ (v._____)

   2._____

   _____ (v._____)

   3._____

   _____ (v._____)

   b. The wise man and the fool are distinguishable by their actions and their speech. What are two characteristics of a fool's speech (Ecclesiastes 5:2; 10:12–14)?

   1. _____

   2. _____

   c. What are some characteristics of wise speech (Ecclesiastes 5:2; 10:12; 12:11; Ephesians 4:29; 5:4)?

   _____

   _____

   _____

8. The Bible commands God's people to obey their government leaders and to resist the temptation to rebel, even if the cause seems just and the leaders appear to be corrupt (Ecclesiastes 8:2–6; Romans 13:1–7). Even if citizens act responsibly, however, incompetent leaders can bring great distress to their people by making foolish decisions (Ecclesiastes 10:16).

Is it time for you to move from being a perpetual learner to a disciple-maker?

ADDITIONAL
INSIGHTS

   a. What two situations can cause a nation to be in great distress (Ecclesiastes 10:16, **woe to you, O land**)?

   1. _____

   2. _____

   b. What two (character) qualities must the government officials exhibit before the nation is called blessed (Ecclesiastes 10:17)?

   1. _____

   2. _____

9. At first glance the statement **Because of laziness the building decays, and through idleness of hands the house leaks** (Ecclesiastes 10:18) appears to be unrelated to the subject of good and bad government. If this verse, however, is related to the discussion on government leadership, it teaches an important truth. What do you think it is?

   _____

   _____

10. When citizens observe political corruption, they're often tempted to become disillusioned and turn their attention to more personal matters of life (making money, etc.; Ecclesiastes 10:19). If Christians find themselves under government leaders who are foolish, how should they respond (Ecclesiastes 10:20; 1 Timothy 2:1–3)?

   _____

   _____

11. What is the most important spiritual truth you learned from this lesson?

_____

_____

_____

_____

TEN

LIVING WITHOUT FEAR

Read Ecclesiastes 11; other references as given.

How should we live in a world where death can come at any time, wisdom and righteousness aren't always rewarded, and oppression and injustice abound? Should we live in fear? Do we abandon pursuing God's wisdom and instead adopt the carnal approach of the hedonist or the mental arrogance of the secular rationalist?

In Ecclesiastes chapter 11, the wise teacher offers some surprisingly practical instruction about living wisely in an uncertain world. The teacher's generous use of living illustrations (bread, clouds, a tree, an unborn baby) isn't designed to obscure his teaching or frustrate his students. Their use creates a subtle resistance to students' initial understanding of truth, forcing them to solve the "word puzzles" before they possess the truth. The time and effort they expend enable them to "own" the truth, which accomplishes the teacher's intended purpose.

Before you begin this lesson, humble yourself before God and ask Him to reveal Himself to you through His inspired Word.

1. There are two interpretations of the truth expressed in Ecclesiastes 11:1–2. The first interpretation teaches that individuals should be generous (**cast your bread upon the waters**; literally, the flatbread of the Middle East can float). The second interpretation refers to diversification in commerce. Since no investment is guaranteed and life is

Many groups study the Final Exam the week after the final lesson for three reasons: (1) someone might come to Christ, (2) believers gain assurance of salvation, (3) group members learn how to share the gospel.

ADD GROUP
INSIGHTS BELOW

uncertain, people should diversify because they have no assurance that a particular business venture will succeed.

a. Which of these interpretations do you believe is the correct one? Why?

_____

_____

_____

b. How can you apply this practical truth to your life?

_____

_____

2. a. An early church leader named Jerome believed the fallen tree pictured man's irreversible destiny after death (Ecclesiastes 11:3). Do you agree with Jerome's interpretation? Please support your answer.

_____

_____

_____

_____

b. Ecclesiastes 11:3 uses two illustrations (clouds full of water and the fallen tree) to teach one important truth about life. What is it?

_____

_____

3. Most people realize that life is unpredictable. How we respond to life's unpredictability is equally predictable. Many people become fearful and cautious, hoping to minimize the chance of failure. Others boldly charge forward to succeed before misfortune knocks at their door.

a. What sound advice does the wise teacher give his listeners regarding how to live in an unpredictable world (Ecclesiastes 11:4)?

_____

_____

b. List at least two ways you intend to apply this important truth to your life.

_____

_____

_____

_____

For more discipleship help, sign up to receive the Disciple-Maker Tips—a bi-monthly email that provides insights to help your small group function more effectively.

ADDITIONAL INSIGHTS

4. There are many things in life man does not know. List the five unknowns identified in Ecclesiastes 11:2–6.

1. _____

_____ (v. _____)

2. _____

_____ (v. _____)

3. _____

_____ (v. _____)

4. _____

_____ (v. _____)

5. _____

_____ (v. _____)

5. It's likely that Jesus Christ had Ecclesiastes 11:5 in mind when he talked with a Pharisee named Nicodemus (John 3:1–8). Just as man cannot understand the way of the wind, Nicodemus couldn't understand the work of the Holy Spirit in salvation.

a. What did Jesus tell Nicodemus that seemed hard for him to understand (John 3:6–7)?

_____

_____

_____

c. Are you certain you understand what it means to be born again?
☐ Yes   ☐ No   ☐ I am not completely sure

If you're not certain, turn to the back of this study guide and read the Final Exam over carefully. It will explain from the Bible how you can receive the gift of eternal life.

6. Ironically man cannot be certain about many things of this life, but he can be certain about where he will spend eternity (1 John 5:11–13). If a man dwells on the things he can't know about this life, he might lose his motivation for living. How should we live, even though we can't know for certain about this life (Ecclesiastes 11:6)?

_____

_____

7. Even though man doesn't know the details of the future, he shouldn't live in fear or defeat. God provides the simple pleasures of food, work, and family to encourage him during his earthly pilgrimage (Ecclesiastes 3:12–13; 9:9). God has also given the sun to brighten his spirits (Ecclesiastes 11:7). Every man chooses his attitude as he responds to the trials and blessings God allows him to experience.

a. Describe the attitude God wants you to possess in life (Ecclesiastes 11:8–10).

_____

_____

b. What phrase instructs you that every man should maintain a joyous attitude throughout life (Ecclesiastes 11:8)?

_____

_____

It's time to order your next study. Allow enough time to get the books so you can distribute them at the Open House. Consider ordering 2-3 extra books for newcomers.

ADDITIONAL
INSIGHTS

8. Many Christians know they shouldn't worry about the future because it robs them of the joy God wants for them. Many, however, feel powerless to stop worrying. From the following verses, list at least four biblical principles that help every Christian overcome worry and enjoy the life God gives (Ecclesiastes 2:26; Philippians 3:13; 4:6, 8; 1 Peter 5:7).

1. _____

   _____ (v. _____)

2. _____

   _____ (v. _____)

3. _____

   _____ (v. _____)

4. _____

   _____ (v. _____)

9. Many people can relate to the phrase **the days of darkness** (Ecclesiastes 11:8). Do you think this phrase refers to (1) death, (2) difficult days in a person's past, or (3) the twilight years of life (Ecclesiastes 11:8)? Why?

_____

_____

_____

10. The book of Ecclesiastes dismantles the non-Christian's hope of finding lasting peace and fulfillment without God. At the same time, the book helps believers understand the mental struggles and inner turmoil of the unsaved. Hopefully,

the book has helped you gain greater compassion for the lost. In the first nine chapters of Ecclesiastes, the wise teacher presented three powerful truths that explain how God works to bring all men to the knowledge of the truth and find lasting joy in life. What are they (Ecclesiastes 3:11, 14, 18)?

_____

_____

_____

_____

ELEVEN

THE PURPOSE OF LIFE

Read Ecclesiastes 12; other references as given.

In the first eleven chapters the wise teacher led his students through a comprehensive analysis of secularism. He concluded that we must acknowledge and fear God to find meaning and happiness because hedonism, humanism, and materialism do not bring lasting satisfaction.

In Ecclesiastes chapter 12, the wise teacher exhorts his listeners to give the best of their lives to God (Ecclesiastes 12:1–7), reminds them one last time of the vanity of life (verse 8), explains his method of teaching (verses 9–12), and makes his final point. Like any good teacher, he presents his students with the right questions, helps them consider all possible answers, and encourages them to accept the truth.

Before you begin, ask God to reveal Himself to you and to transform you into the image of His Son.

Final Exam:

Are you meeting next week to study the Final Exam? To learn how to present it effectively, go to www.Lamplighters USA.org/training.

———

ADD GROUP INSIGHTS BELOW

1. In Ecclesiastes 11, the wise teacher instructs his listeners to rejoice in life while they are young enough to enjoy it (Ecclesiastes 11:8–10). Beginning in chapter 12, he tells his audience to remember the Creator before **the difficult days come** (Ecclesiastes 12:1). The theological meaning of the Hebrew word for **remember** (*zakar*) means "more than mere mental cognizance or recollection" (Hebrews 12:1).

   a. The same Hebrew word is used in Genesis 19:29 and 1 Samuel 1:11, 19–20. How can we know from these two passages that the Hebrew word *zakar* in this context means more than mere recollection?

_____

_____

b. Now that you have a more complete understanding of the Hebrew word for "remember," restate the command in Ecclesiastes 12:1 in your own words, capturing the meaning of the Hebrew word *zakar*.

_____

_____

_____

c. What practical steps do you think a Christian should take to **remember now your Creator in the days of your youth** (Ecclesiastes 12:1)?

_____

_____

_____

_____

2. From the immediate context it's easy to see that **difficult days** (NIV, "days of trouble") refers to the elderly years of life (Ecclesiastes 12:1–7). Why do you think they're referred to as such?

_____

_____

_____

3. The wise teacher uses vivid imagery to describe many of the characteristics of old age (Ecclesiastes 12:3–6). What aspects of old age do you think the following phrases signify?

a. The keepers of the house tremble (Ecclesiastes 12:3).

_____

_____

Would you like to learn how to solve all small group problems? Contact Lamplighters to learn how.

ADDITIONAL INSIGHTS

b. The grinders cease because they are few (Ecclesiastes 12:3). _____

_____

c. Those who look through windows (the Hebrew word for *look through* means "holes") grow dim (Ecclesiastes 12:3). _____

_____

d. The doors are shut and the sound of grinding is low (Ecclesiastes 12:4). _____

_____

e. One rises up at the sound of a bird (Ecclesiastes 12:4).

_____

_____

f. The almond tree blossoms (Ecclesiastes 12:5).

_____

_____

g. The grasshopper is a burden (Ecclesiastes 12:5, NIV, "drags himself along").

_____

_____

h. The desire fails (Ecclesiastes 12:5).

_____

_____

4. a. The wise teacher's figurative language pictures the inevitable culmination of man's earthly existence, which is death (Ecclesiastes 12:6). To what do you think the **silver cord** refers (Ecclesiastes 12:6)?

    _____

    _____

    b. Looking at life from the perspective of **under the sun**, the wise teacher indicates that death is the end of everything (Ecclesiastes 3:19). By this he means that men's earthly hope and dreams will forever cease at the time of death. Only occasionally did he refer to a reality beyond the grave (Ecclesiastes 3:15; 12:7). What happens to all men after they die (Ecclesiastes 12:7; Hebrews 9:27)?

    _____

    _____

5. Some interpreters take exception to Solomon calling himself wise (Ecclesiastes 12:9). Solomon, however, identifies himself as functioning in an official capacity of a sage, or teacher (Jeremiah 18:18). As a sage, he fulfilled several responsibilities of a wise teacher. Name at least four (Ecclesiastes 12: 9–10).

    1. _____

    2. _____

    3. _____

    4. _____

6. a. What do you think is the meaning of the phrase "sought to find delightful words" (Ecclesiastes 12:10 NASB)?

    _____

    _____

b. What is a goad (Ecclesiastes 12:11), and in what ways do you think the Word of God should be like a goad?

_____

_____

_____

Would you like to learn how to lead someone through this same study? It's not hard. Go to www.Lamplighters USA.org to register for *free* online leadership training.

ADDITIONAL INSIGHTS

7. The phrase **well-driven nails** perhaps refers to nails or tent pegs driven by shepherds to secure their tents (Ecclesiastes 12:11). If this is true, what do you think is being taught by this simile?

_____

_____

_____

8. a. Many nonbelievers think Ecclesiastes is nothing more than a compilation of several writers' opinions on various life issues. What proof does the book of Ecclesiastes offer that refutes their assessment?

_____

_____

b. Who is this Shepherd (Psalm 80:1)?

_____

9. a. What is the grand conclusion of the wise teacher's search for meaning and fulfillment in life (Ecclesiastes 12:13)?

_____

_____

b. Why should everyone fear God and keep His commandments (Ecclesiastes 12:13–14)?

_____

10. What are the three most important truths you learned from your study of the book of Ecclesiastes?

1. _____

_____ (v. _____)

2. _____

_____ (v. _____)

3. _____

_____ (v. _____)

Be prepared to share your answers with the other members of your group if you feel comfortable.

LEADER'S GUIDE

Lesson 1: Life Is Meaningless

1. The wise teacher presents life from the perspective of a natural (unsaved) man who is attempting to find meaning and happiness in life apart from God. He addresses the general public, whose view of life is limited by what they can see, touch, and understand. The wise teacher meets them on their ground and proceeds to convict them of their vain attempts to find meaning in life. Ecclesiastes is a critique of secularism and secularized religion.

2. a. The phrase "under the sun" means the writer is viewing life from an earthly viewpoint devoid of an eternal perspective.
    b. 1. Wisdom literature addresses the practical aspects of life.
        2. Wisdom literature makes frequent use of questions without providing immediate answers.
        3. Wisdom literature addresses some of man's most complex questions.

3. a. Ecclesiastes helps unsaved people in general realize that life without God leads only to vanity and emptiness.
    b. Ecclesiastes helps Christians understand the confusion that those without Christ live with on a daily basis. By understanding the mind-set of the unsaved, the believer's heart, often cold and uncaring about the lost, is warned with an increased compassion for their plight. The believer is motivated to reach the lost with the gospel of Jesus Christ so they can escape their emptiness, understand the meaning of life, and experience the joy of knowing Jesus Christ.

4. a. Everything in life that's not centered on God leads to emptiness. Life without Christ cannot provide lasting satisfaction or fulfillment.
    b. Answers will vary. A possible suggestion: There is no enduring satisfaction and fulfillment (profit) in life if man focused his energy entirely on self-centered goals.

5. a. The wise teacher wrote from an earthly perspective. From man's perspective, it appears that the earth will last forever. When viewing life from a human perspective, the earth appears to be an immovable, eternal object. Man appears to be in a continual state of turmoil and transition from one generation to the next.

   b. 1. He compared the transitory nature of man and the passing of endless generations to the apparent permanence of the earth (Ecclesiastes 1:4).

   2. He spoke of the sun rising, setting, and hastening to the place where it rises again (Ecclesiastes 1:5). When he spoke of the sun rising and setting, he was speaking in "geocentric" terms. Meteorologists use this same language when they say the sun is rising and setting during the day. When they do this, they are speaking from the perspective of the law of observation. It is the earth that is actually rotating, but from man's perspective, it looks like the sun is rising and setting. The wise teacher said the sun hastened to the place where it rises again. When life is viewed from man's perspective, it's almost as if he thinks no one is on the other side of the earth—another indication of a man-centered perspective on life.

   3. He spoke of the wind turning toward the south, the north, and completing its circuit as if it acted on its own volition. From man's perspective, the wind's chaotic and unpredictable manner doesn't seem to be controlled by an omniscient God (Matthew 8:27).

   4. He spoke of rivers running into the seas/oceans, but they never seem to be full (Ecclesiastes 1:7). Man can't see the evaporation of the seas which causes water to eventually return to land.

6. a. 1. The natural man cannot receive the things of God.
      2. Man cannot comprehend the things of God.
   b. Answers will vary.

7. a. The wise teacher spoke of human wisdom because it leads to emptiness, grief, and sorrow (Ecclesiastes 1:17–18). God's wisdom leads to peace and joy.
   b. 1. Human wisdom has been exposed as foolishness by God (1 Corinthians 1:20).

2. Human wisdom is incapable of helping us know God (1 Corinthians 1:21).
3. Human wisdom is inferior to God's wisdom (1 Corinthians 1:25).

8. a. Human wisdom can identify the great questions of life, but it cannot provide tangible answers to the critical questions in life (How was the world created? What is the meaning of life? What happens after death?). Human wisdom sees the problems, but it isn't able to find the answers. Having unanswered questions is always a painful and frustrating endeavor, especially when those questions and answers are at the core of man's existence and the meaning in life.
   b. Mental/emotional.

9. He must be born again (born of the Spirit).

10. Answers will vary.

Lesson 2: Pleasure Doesn't Satisfy

1. Pleasure.

2. a. Luke 15:12   Rebellion (separation from accountability)
   b. Luke 15:13   Riotous (sinful) living
   c. Luke 15:14–16 Ruination (due to God's chastening)
   d. Luke 15:17   Repentance
   e. Luke 15:18   Reconciliation

3. a. Personal achievement or career and business success.
   b. 1. He said it was empty.
      2. He said it's like grasping the wind, which meant it was elusive with nothing substantial to hold on to at the end of the journey.
      3. He said he gained no lasting or fulfilling benefit from his endeavors.

4. a. "I," "myself"
   b. "I"
   c. Answers will vary.

5. a. 1. Wisdom is better than folly (Ecclesiastes 2:13).
   2. Wisdom illuminates a man's path through life (Ecclesiastes 2:14).
   3. Wisdom has no advantage over folly when it comes to death (Ecclesiastes 2:14–15).

   b. He hated life because everything was empty and said it was like trying to grasp the wind (Ecclesiastes 2:17). He was speaking from the perspective of someone living "under the sun."

   c. Answers will vary.

6. Just as grasping for or chasing after the wind is a useless endeavor, trying to find satisfaction in life apart from God is equally futile. There is no place to find the source of the wind, and there is no place for man to find true meaning and satisfaction in this world apart from God.

7. a. 1. He hated life because he had to leave everything to his successor who might lose all he gained by his own efforts (Ecclesiastes 2:18–19).
   2. He changed his thinking regarding the significance of his work and fell into despair because all his work might be lost (Ecclesiastes 2:20–21).
   3. He reevaluated man's struggles and strenuous efforts and concluded that it's all vanity and emptiness (Ecclesiastes 2:22–23).

   b. Answers will vary.

8. 1. Man should enjoy his work and find satisfaction in it. If he can do this, it's a gift from God (Ecclesiastes 2:24).
   2. Everyone can experience the same amount of enjoyment in life if they're properly aligned with God (Ecclesiastes 2:25–26a).
   3. God gives wisdom, knowledge, and joy to those who live according to His will (Ecclesiastes 2:26).
   4. God redistributes the goods of this world, taking from those who do not submit to His plan and giving to those who follow His ways (Ecclesiastes 2:26).

9. Answers will vary.

Lesson 3: A Time for Everything

1. Realities of life. God's plan for man didn't include some of these characteristics. It seems best to view them as results of living in a fallen world cursed by sin. God allows them during this time, or He wouldn't permit them to happen.

2. a. The "just war" theory began in ancient Greek society and was developed further by a number of Christian theologians. To be considered a "just war," five criteria must be met: (1) Just Cause — there must be a just cause to engage in war, such as self-defense or defense of a weaker nation where innocent people are being killed. (2) Formal Declaration — an official declaration of war must be made by a proper authority. (3) Right Intention — the motive for going to war must be just, such as establishing peace. Revenge and mere political expansion are not just causes. (4) Legitimate Possibility of Success — a nation that goes to war must have a reasonable chance of success, or its citizens will die needlessly. (5) Proportionality — the use of military might must not be excessive, resulting in unnecessary death and destruction.

   b. Capital punishment is clearly taught in both the Old and New Testaments (Genesis 9:6; Romans 13:4). The apostle Paul said he was willing to be put to death at the hands of the state if he had done something worthy of capital punishment (Acts 25:11). The Bible teaches that lawlessness increases when justice is not meted out swiftly (Ecclesiastes 8:11).

3. a. In some situations, we do play God. The advancement of life-sustaining medical technology and society's continuing inability to define when life begins (at conception or at birth) and ends (the cessation of voluntary respiratory function, the discontinuation of detectable brain wave function, etc.) have forced man to face ethical questions he has never had to face in the past. Some families have been advised to discontinue a loved one's basic needs (food and water) because death is imminent, quality of life is significantly impaired, or the patient's recovery is extremely unlikely. When we attempt to define life based on the quality-of-life factor rather than viewing life as a gift from God, we're likely to make critical health care decisions that may be inconsistent with God's will.

b. Man doesn't have the right to take another person's life because the Bible says, "You shall not murder" (Exodus 20:13).

c. No. God has appointed a time for everything, including death (Ecclesiastes 3:1–2). Using extraordinary medical procedures often prolongs life rather than causing death. In many situations, the decision to not incorporate heroic medical procedures to save a patient doesn't constitute murder or a lack of love. It's simply recognizing that life has predictable and unavoidable cycles ("a time to die").

4. 1. Matthew 5:28: God condemns lust as a sin and equates it with committing adultery. Being tempted is not lusting, but temptation often leads to lust and lust to immoral behavior. Lust is a sin that occurs when an individual embraces sexual temptation mentally, regardless whether he or she acts upon it.

   2. Romans 1:26–27: Homosexuality is a sin.

   3. 1 Corinthians 5:11: Christians are commanded not to associate with another Christian who is involved in habitual sexual sin.

   4. 1 Corinthians 6:18: Christians are to flee from sexual immorality.

   5. 1 Thessalonians 4:3: It's God's will for every believer to be morally pure.

5. It refers to the time when individuals should put away their grief and resume their God-given responsibilities.

6. The wise teacher says God has a sovereign, eternal plan that can neither be changed nor completely understood by anyone during their lifetime (Ecclesiastes 3:11). He believes one's joy in life is related to the work God assigns him, even though he doesn't fully comprehend what God is doing. If you enjoy your work and do good, you may be receiving the ultimate earthly satisfaction (Ecclesiastes 3:12–13). He believed joy, enjoyment of one's work, and the simple pleasures of life are gifts from God (Ecclesiastes 3:13).

7. a. God places the reality of eternity in every person's heart. The Hebrew word (ha' olam) represents "everness" and occurs in Ecclesiastes 1:4 and 12:5. The use of the definite article indicates that the whole of eternity, rather than particular ages, is in view. The knowledge that God places in man's heart enables him to anticipate some measure of

human reality beyond the grave. This gives him the ability to consider the eternal dimension of life and the transitory nature of this physical world.

b. 1. Evangelism is not convincing others of the reality of God and eternity. It's reminding them of a truth that God has already placed in their hearts (the concept of eternality) and telling them what God wants them to know (the gospel of Jesus Christ).

2. As we grow older and the daily responsibilities of life diminish, the reality of eternity remains in our thinking and often becomes more dominant as we get closer to eternity. There's a common misconception in the church that as a man grows older, the chances decrease that he might be saved. This error denies the truth of Ecclesiastes 3:11 and is inconsistent with the numerous biblical accounts of conversion testimonies, which are almost all adults.

8. a. So that man might fear and revere God.

b. Both problems and trials are part of God's plan. They're divinely arranged by God's loving hand to help us learn to fear Him.

9. 1. Corrupt government workers, such as politicians, judges, lawyers, and law enforcement officers, who use their position for personal gain rather than the betterment of people and the glory of God ("in the place of judgment, wickedness was there"). Other answers could apply.

2. Religious leaders (pastors, elders, priests, television evangelists, etc.) who use their position of authority and respect to take advantage of others ("in the place of righteousness, iniquity was there"). Other answers could apply.

10. Men are like animals from the perspective that they both eventually die. Ecclesiastes 3:19–20 proves that duration of life is in view.

11. a. When viewing life from an earthly perspective ("under the sun"), man seems to have no specific advantage over the beasts, even in death. If life exists only on earth and there is no future resurrection, men and beasts experience the same fate (physical death) because they die in a similar manner.

b. The conclusion is that man has no advantage over beasts if there is no afterlife. Jehovah's Witnesses use this passage as a proof text to support their erroneous doctrine of "soul sleep." They fail to recognize that Ecclesiastes is written from a human perspective ("under the sun"). If life is lived from an earthly perspective, the only thing any of us can do is to enjoy the things we do (Ecclesiastes 3:22). The wise teacher is giving a very bleak picture of the lives of unsaved people. They don't know the meaning of life, they don't know God, they don't know whether there is an afterlife or where they will spend eternity. The only thing they can do is rejoice in their work(s). It has been said that if a person is unsaved, this (this life) is the best he will ever have it, and if a person is saved, this is the worst he will ever have it.

Lesson 4: The Sacrifice of Fools

1. a. 1. Oppression of people is a reality of life (Ecclesiastes 4:1).
   2. Oppression usually comes from those who have the power to exploit others (Ecclesiastes 4:1).
   3. Oppression hurts people, and sometimes there is no one to help or comfort the oppressed (Ecclesiastes 4:2).
   b. It would be better to be dead or else never to have been born than see all the oppression in this world (Ecclesiastes 4:2–3).

2. a. Envy.
   b. Laziness.

3. He failed to consider the real purpose for his efforts and to whom he would leave his fortune if he had no children or family. The wise teacher said this was vanity.

4. 1. Two (or more) people working together can often accomplish more than two people working independently (Ecclesiastes 4:9).
   2. People who work together can help each other in a time of misfortune, such as illness, injury, or accident (Ecclesiastes 4:10).
   3. People who work together can provide something that others need (Ecclesiastes 4:11).
   4. People who work together can support each other when opposition arises (Ecclesiastes 4:12).

5. a. The old, foolish king had stopped learning.
   b. 1. The king demonstrated the tendency for people to become less teachable as they grow older.
      2. People can quickly change their allegiance from one person to another (Ecclesiastes 4:15–16).

6. a. 1. Walk prudently, or guard your steps, as you go into the house of God.
      2. Draw near to listen.
   b. The sacrifice of fools is the thoughtless and irreverent ritualistic "worship" some people offer to God. The word *rather* (Ecclesiastes 5:1) indicates that the sacrifice of fools is characterized by an irreverent approach to God and an unwillingness to listen. The fool's religious sacrifice is also characterized by a lack of spiritual humility before God, vain and meaningless prayers, and the conspicuous absence of contemplative spiritual reflection. It's called the sacrifice of fools because those who worship in this manner don't realize their worship is unacceptable to God. This kind of worship displeases and dishonors God and will be exposed ultimately as the sacrifice of fools.

7. A Christian should prepare himself physically, mentally, and spiritually to corporately worship God. He should guard himself against everything (thoughts, activities, etc.) that distract from the true worship of God. The verb tense of the Hebrew word *shamar* (imperative) makes it a command, indicating the individual must honor God in worship rather than offering the sacrifice of fools.

8. a. Ecclesiastes 5:2 — I will quiet my heart and limit my speech before God and others as I prepare to worship.
   b. Ecclesiastes 5:4 — I will not make promises (vows) to God that I don't intend to fulfill.
   c. Ecclesiastes 5:6 — I will be careful and accurate in what I say to others.
   d. Ecclesiastes 5:7 — I will fear God and walk with Him. Other answers could apply.

9. The Christian's body.

10. No, but a Christian should be careful about making a vow about the future over which we have no control. Matthew 5:33–37 and James 5:12 indicate that

it's wrong to vow, but there's biblical evidence to the contrary (2 Corinthians 1:23; Galatians 1:20). The Mosaic law forbade irreverent oaths and lightly using the Lord's name to attest to one's honesty (Exodus 20:7; Leviticus 19:12). Once Yahweh's name was invoked, the vow became a debt that was owed not only to another individual but also to the Lord (Ecclesiastes 5:4). In ancient Israel the people developed a sophisticated scheme to judge how binding an oath really was by examining its relationship to Yahweh's name. An Israelite could swear by heaven, by earth, or by Jerusalem, but he could not swear toward Jerusalem. Jesus Christ confronted their deceptive communication by eliminating oaths; He stated that an individual's words should be honest without having to be affirmed by an oath. It should be noted that Paul's calling of God as His witness to his soul was to affirm something that had happened in the past, not something in the future over which he had no control. A believer should be careful not to make vows about the future, and he should enter into a vow fully cognizant of his continuing responsibility. (Wedding vows are not wrong as long as individuals realize the seriousness of them, and they commit themselves to faithfully fulfilling them, even if their marriage doesn't turn out to be what they hoped.)

11. The believer shouldn't be shocked by injustice. Government officials watch over each other and are accountable to one another (Ecclesiastes 5:8).

12. a. 1. Those who love money will not be satisfied (Ecclesiastes 5:10).
     2. Those who love money will be led into temptation, snares, desires, and passions that may eventually ruin them (1 Timothy 6:9).
   b. 1. They are not in a right relationship with God, and He withholds peace from them to help them realize their mistake and enter into a right relationship with Him.
     2. Deep down in their hearts they know that their wealth can be lost at any time, and this brings a measure of anxiety into their lives.
     3. They know they can die at any time and all can be lost. Other answers could apply.

13. 1. Man can find a measure of joy in the simple pleasures of life such as eating (Ecclesiastes 5:18).
   2. Man can find a measure of joy in the work he accomplishes (Ecclesiastes 5:18–19).

Lesson 5: Work Doesn't Satisfy

1. a. A rich man has accumulated great wealth, but he's not able to enjoy all he has accumulated.
    b. 1. A rich man might lose everything he's gained because of a war or a government seizure of personal property (communism).
        2. A rich man might lose everything he's accumulated by a sudden business failure, lawsuit, or ruinous business decision.
        3. A rich man might lose everything he's accumulated through an injury, accident, or illness that prevents him from managing his financial affairs properly and enjoying his success.
        4. Other answers could apply.
2. a. 1. The man had many children and a long life, but he was not satisfied.
        2. The man did not have a proper burial. The Bible doesn't say whether the man's poverty or his children's failure to honor him in death were the cause of the improper burial.
    b. The miscarriage, because a miscarried child never sees the sun (Ecclesiastes 6:5).

3. a. Obedience to God and His Word in all aspects of life.
    b. Career success, interpersonal relationships, money, entertainment. Other answers could apply.
    c. Answers will vary.

4. a. 1. He almost lost sight of His devotion and commitment to the Lord (Psalm 73:2, "my feet had almost stumbled").
        2. He became envious of the wealth of the boastful (Psalm 73:3).
        3. He doubted God's omniscience (Psalm 73:11).
        4. He began to doubt whether it was worthwhile to serve God (Psalm 73:13–14).
        5. He lost spiritual joy (Psalm 73:16).
    b. Asaph regained a biblical perspective when he saw the situation from God's perspective (Psalm 73:17). He realized that the success of the wicked was precarious (verse 18, "You [God] set them in slippery places"), and they would eventually be destroyed if they didn't repent (verses 19, 27). He realized that God would never forsake him (verse 23), and His counsel would continue to guide him until he was received into His presence (verse 24). When Asaph saw this entire situation

from God's perspective, he realized that his former thoughts had been senseless and ignorant (verse 22). When he turned his eyes back on the Lord, communion with God became his greatest desire, and he stopped envying others and coveting their situation (verse 26).

5. Answers will vary but could include the following. God designed the reproductive systems of men and women to produce children for an extended period. For some couples, the question of having more children has been settled by health-related reproductive problems. Many Christian couples, however, are able to have more children, and the question of birth control, either temporary or permanent, becomes an important ethical question. It may be wise for a Christian couple to discuss their thoughts and concerns with each other and with their pastor. Also, if they're convinced that birth control isn't wrong, they should carefully examine various types of birth control to make sure they choose a method that prevents fertilization rather than one that functions as an abortifacient. Some Christian couples base their decision to have more children on finances, failing to remember that God always provides for His people.

6. 1. All men (wise or foolish) eventually end up in the grave (Ecclesiastes 6:6).
    2. All men (wise or foolish) who labor for themselves will never be satisfied (v. 7). The word *wise* is used in this passage (Ecclesiastes 6:8) to describe an intelligent man who acts prudently, even though he might not be saved. He has no real advantage over the fool because he labors only for temporal benefits ("all a man's labor is for his mouth") and does not find satisfaction.

7. Answers will vary.

8. A believer can be assured that he will experience lasting fulfillment and satisfaction in life if he or she is rightly aligned with God. Specifically, he must be seeking to know God and His Word (be walking with God) and seek to know God's will and submit to it on a moment-by-moment basis.

9. a. 1. The nature and essence of man, including his limitations, are foreordained by God (Ecclesiastes 6:10).
        2. God is mightier than man, so it's futile for him to argue or contend with God (Ecclesiastes 6:10b).

3. Both man's time on earth and his perspective on life are so limited that his life appears as a fleeting shadow, and he has no idea what will happen on earth after his death (Ecclesiastes 6:12).

b. Answers will vary.

10. Answers will vary.

Lesson 6: True Righteousness

1. A person with a "good name" has a good reputation among those who know the difference between good and bad character. While it probably indicates that his or her life is characterized by virtuous conduct, a good name doesn't always refer to a person's character. Reputation is what people think you are; character is what God knows you are.

2. 1. The deceased person's struggle through life is finally over.
   2. Those who attend the funeral are reminded of the reality of death and their own finality. It is better for someone to go to a funeral than a party because those who attend the funeral think about their mortality.

3. These are all the places where the "god" of pleasure is promoted and God's name and His ways are not revered. Although it naturally includes places such as bars, it could include becoming engaged in the drug culture, as well as becoming addicted to things such as food, immoral behavior/sex, fashion—literally anything that captures our hearts and affections and take us away from God.

4. a. 1. The fool's focus in life is on pleasure (Ecclesiastes 7:4).
   2. The fool's speech is empty and devoid of significant contribution to others (Ecclesiastes 7:5).
   3. The fool's laughter is nothing but noise (Ecclesiastes 7:6).
   4. The fool's life is often characterized by anger (Ecclesiastes 7:9).
   b. Answers will vary.
   c. Answers will vary.
   d. Answers will vary.

5. 1 In times of prosperity, it's okay to rejoice in your good fortune and God's blessing.

   2. In times of adversity, remember that God has appointed difficult times as well as prosperous times.

   3. A believer can't know God's plan regarding why or how He allows times of prosperity and adversity or what will happen after we die.

6. Sometimes godly people die prematurely, and some wicked people live long lives. If unsaved people recognize this as an injustice in life, they are unwittingly acknowledging the distinction between righteousness and wickedness, even though they're unwilling to yield their lives to God's control.

7. The wise teacher is presenting a view of life from a natural, earthly perspective. Because the natural man cannot comprehend the eternal dimension of life, he cannot understand why a righteous person would live a godly life if he has no guarantee of a long life. He doesn't realize that the righteous live for eternal rewards, not temporal benefits. To the unsaved man, the godly man's life looks excessively righteous if the only observable reward of doing right (a prolonged life) isn't always realized. This verse might also teach that an incorrect form of righteousness (excessive) leads to spiritual ruin. This form of "righteousness" is man-centered, flesh-driven, and conspicuously absent of God's grace. Many Christians live for God in their own strength rather than in God's power. The results are often a lack of genuine joy, an ineffective witness for Christ, and a judgmental attitude toward other members of the body of Christ.

8. a. Answers will vary but could include the following:

   1. They embrace faulty plans for spiritual growth such as religious psychology, legalism, mysticism, or asceticism (Colossians 2:20–23).

   2. They lack full understanding of God's forgiveness of their past sins. They serve God out of guilt rather than out of love for Jesus Christ who died for their sins. This is a form of spiritual penance.

   3. If they were saved later in life, they might believe they should make up for all the time they served the devil and be caught in "performance" Christianity. Other answers could apply.

   b. 1. Some religious zealots become social recluses, or they journey to distant lands to find God. They often treat their bodies severely, believing God will look favorably on their self-inflicted asceticism.

2. Christians who are unable to comprehend God's plan for spiritual growth may adopt lengthy lists of personal convictions that are not scriptural. Legalism takes their spiritual attention off Jesus Christ. Many believers experience unnecessary emotional and family problems because they practice a faulty form of righteousness.

9. Practical righteousness. The last phrase in the verse describes the one who is not righteous. He is not righteous because he's unable to continually do good and not sin. Both positional righteousness and ultimate righteousness are instantaneous gifts from God that are not dependent on an individual's continuing obedience to God.

10. A Christian shouldn't take everything other people say about him too seriously. The word *everything* (NIV, "every word") is the key interpretive word in these verses. Although a believer should be open to comments, suggestions, and critiques of others, he shouldn't be overly sensitive to what is said about him because he might become discouraged. If a believer is preoccupied with what others say about him, he will not be sensitive to God and His Word.

11. a. 1. Man is unable to live wisely (apart from God), even though he desires to do so (Ecclesiastes 7:23).
    2. Man cannot understand the ancient mysteries of the universe, even though he diligently tries to discover them (Ecclesiastes 7:24–25).

    b. A believer will escape the snares of the ungodly.

12. a. Solomon chose to have many wives and concubines. While many of these marriages were probably only political alliances, his decision to marry many women likely kept him from developing a close relationship with any of them. He couldn't meet their needs, so he began to resent them rather than understanding his own mistake.

    b. God created man to be upright in thinking and physical structure, but man chose to go his own independent way. God gave man a measure of free will, and man uses this freedom to pervert God's original intent for his life. Some Bible commentators see a reference to man's rejection of God's original design of being upright. The evolutionist's desire to make man part of the evolutionary process reduces man to an evolving animal that isn't accountable to a holy God.

Lesson 7: Who Is Wise?

1. a. Wisdom illuminates a man's countenance because he finds answers to the important questions in life.
   b. When an individual is in a right relationship with God, first in salvation and second in spiritual growth, he's able to understand how God is working in and through his life for His glory and his good. If a Christian walks with God in this way, he will have constant joy regardless of the circumstances he faces because he knows God is in control, and his sole responsibility is to respond to His leading and rejoice in His goodness. How could this not make a person's face to shine if he knows and experiences the greatest secret of life—Christ in you, the hope of glory?

2. a. Answers will vary.
   b. Answers will vary.

3. Christians should obey the God-ordained government He has placed over them. This includes those authorities that are ungodly and unjust (Romans 13:1). Since God is sovereign and He has ordained human government, a Christian should realize that government officials are ministers of God. When a Christian resists the government authority that God has placed over him, he is resisting the Lord. This is why the Bible says believers ought to obey for conscience's sake (Romans 13:5).

4. The wise teacher is stating a general truth, not an absolute promise. If a Christian shows respect and honor and obeys the laws of the land, he can have confidence that nothing harmful will happen to him.

5. a. Christians should obey the government God has placed over them (Ecclesiastes 8:2; Romans 13:1). God has ordained human government

to effectively administrate society. Even though government officials often make unwise decisions, God expects His people to obey them.

b. Christians shouldn't be quick to reject the government's authority or become part of an insurgency (Ecclesiastes 8:3) because government has the power and authority to inflict punishment (Ecclesiastes 8:3–4). If a government is unjust or political oppression becomes severe, they are to wait patiently for God's leading regarding how and when to act according to His leading (Ecclesiastes 8:6).

c. The same principle of patience and caution can be rightfully applied to a hostile work environment.

6. 1. No one can accurately predict what will happen and when certain things will occur (Ecclesiastes 8:7).

2. Rebellious actions against civil authority could lead to death (Ecclesiastes 8:8).

7. There's no lasting memory of those who die. While the memories of some noteworthy people have extended beyond the grave, the wise teacher spoke about a general principle. Most people can give only scant information about the generations that lived before them. The wise teacher's willingness to link the faded memory of the wicked and the righteous indicates he is reflecting on this problem from an earthly perspective. The testimony of the righteous might be forgotten in a primary sense, but their testimony lives in the lives of those influenced by them.

8. a. The general principle is that the life of the righteous (those who fear God) on earth will be better than the life of the wicked. Even though there is no guarantee that all will go well for the believer, those who live for God will be rewarded with His blessing here on earth.

b. 1. The fear of man brings a snare (Proverbs 29:25). This means the person is caught is the trap (snare) of finding acceptance with the world (its values, goals, etc.) and therefore unable to serve God. The individual was essentially captured by the world.

2. If a Christian fears man more than God, he will not be a servant of God (Galatians 1:10). To fear God openly means that a believer is not ashamed of Jesus Christ, and he lives courageously for Him in every aspect of life.

9. a. The wise teacher is stating a general truth, not an absolute promise.
    b. The one who lives under the sun should eat, drink, and be merry. This is the highest satisfaction he will achieve in this life if he is not saved. God gives him this much in life, and that is all he can expect.
    c. Answers will vary.

10. a. Cannot/will not find the work (of God).
    b. Answers will vary.

11. Answers will vary.

Lesson 8: Time and Chance

1. 1. All men, saved and unsaved, are under God's control (Ecclesiastes 9:1–2, "their works are in the hand of God").
    2. No man knows his own future (Ecclesiastes 9:1).
    3. All men eventually suffer the same fate (death, Ecclesiastes 9:2).
    4. The hearts of men are full of evil, and madness is in their hearts (Ecclesiastes 9:3). This insanity is the foolishness of man that continues to motivate him to reject God and His sovereign control over the affairs of life.

2. a. All men are sinners (Ecclesiastes 7:20), and the hearts of men are full of evil (Ecclesiastes 9:3).
    b. There is no one on earth who is righteous. In his natural condition, man doesn't understand or seek God. All have turned away from God and are unprofitable to Him (Romans 3:10–12).
    c. In his natural state, man is spiritually dead because of his trespasses and sins. He lives according to the values and principles of this world, which is orchestrated by Satan. He appropriately could be called a son of disobedience because he conducts his life according to the lusts of his flesh. He satisfies his fleshly appetite and carnal mind, and he is just like everyone else—under God's wrath. He's without Christ, even though he may be religious. He's an alien and stranger to the promises and covenants God gave Israel that still apply to Christians. He has no hope apart from Christ saving him, and he is without God in this world.

3. 1. Man's heart (Jeremiah 17:9; that is, the center of his very being, which is often thought to be a combination of his mind, will, and emotions).
    2. Man's body (Romans 8:10).
    3. Man's mind (2 Corinthians 4:4; that is, his intellect, or his ability to understand God and respond to His will).

4. There is hope for all the living, but death ends every goal and dream. Even the most miserable creature, such as a mongrel dog, has more hope than something that is dead. The dead have no consciousness of physical life and no opportunity for future reward, and even their memory is forgotten (Ecclesiastes 9:5). They no longer have an opportunity to enjoy life's simple pleasures (Ecclesiastes 9:6).

5. 1. We should enjoy the simple pleasures of life with a good attitude (Ecclesiastes 9:7).
    2. We should live righteously (Ecclesiastes 9:8).
    3. We should each enjoy our relationship with our spouse (Ecclesiastes 9:9).
    4. We should do our work heartily because a time is coming when the opportunity to be productive will be gone (Ecclesiastes 9:10).

6. Answers will vary. The shorter catechism of the Westminster Confession says it well: The chief end of man is to glorify God and enjoy His presence forever.

7. a. 1. Time and chance overtake every man (Ecclesiastes 9:11). Man has no guarantee that life will turn out the way he hoped or planned. Chance is viewed as merely good or bad luck from the perspective of the unsaved, but it is the unveiling of God's sovereign plan to man.
       2. Death comes at any time, often when we don't expect it (Ecclesiastes 9:12).
    b. Answers will vary.

8. He didn't anticipate his premature death and had not prepared for eternity.

9. Answers will vary, but could include the following:
    1. He should have an up-to-date will.

2. He should adequately prepare financially to provide for his family.
3. He should communicate with his family any specific desires he has regarding funeral arrangements, etc.

Other answers could apply.

10. Answers will vary, but they could include the following: A Christian should enjoy life and the gifts God gives. He should trust God completely in all things. His joyous, grateful heart should reflect his faith in God's sovereignty and goodness. He should live his brief life trusting God and knowing he will not understand everything God does.

11. 1. Strength (Ecclesiastes 9:16).
    2. The shouting of a ruler among fools (Ecclesiastes 9:17).
    3. Weapons of war (Ecclesiastes 9:18).

12. Answers will vary.

Lesson 9: Risk and Reward

1. A single act of folly can adversely affect a man's life and testimony. Just as a few dead flies can ruin an entire fragrant perfume, God's people must think, speak, and act wisely in every situation so their lives aren't tarnished by a single act of folly.

2. a. Achan. He stole some of the spoils ("accursed things") that were taken from the battle of Jericho, even though the Israelites were forbidden to do so (Joshua 7:1). (The phrase *accursed things* meant those things that were wholly dedicated to God and couldn't be used for common or personal use.)
    b. Saul. He spared King Agag and some of the sheep, even though he had been commanded by God to destroy them (1 Samuel 15:14–15). He was rejected as the king for this act of disobedience (1 Samuel 15:26). Note: Although the phrase *accursed things* is not used in this passage, God had dedicated the Amalekites for destruction because of their previous sin against His people (1 Samuel 15:2–3).
    c. David. He committed adultery with a married woman named Bathsheba (2 Samuel 11:4). God said that the sword (hostility, conflict, death, etc.)

would never depart from David's family as a punishment for his sin (2 Samuel 12:10).

d. Cephas (Peter). In Antioch, Peter acted hypocritically by submitting to the Old Testament dietary laws only when the Jews were present (Galatians 2:12). Because of his hypocrisy, other Jewish Christians were also led into error.

3. a. God's Word assures believers they will never stumble if they allow these eight spiritual qualities in their lives (2 Peter 1:10).

   b. Faith, virtue (NIV. "goodness"), knowledge, self-control, perseverance, godliness, brotherly kindness, love (2 Peter 1:5–7).

   c. Answers will vary.

   d. 1. He forfeits the privilege of being useful to God (2 Peter 1:8).

      2. He forfeits the opportunity of being fruitful in his service to God (2 Peter 1:8).

      3. He forfeits the ability to trust God or live by faith (2 Peter 1:9, "blind or shortsighted").

      4. He forfeits the assurance of his salvation (v. 9, "having forgotten his purification from his former sins"). (Believers may lose the assurance of salvation, but not their salvation. The Bible teaches that every believer is secure, but not every believer has the assurance of salvation.)

4. a. 1. It signifies a place of safety and security from God (Psalm 16:8; 121:5).

      2. It signifies a place of confidence and faith in God (Psalm 110:5).

   b. The fool's heart directs him away from the safety and security that God wants to provide for him. The fool's heart directs him to place his trust or confidence in things other than God (his own reasoning, strengths, or experiences; the humanistic teachings of other men, etc.).

5. The one being attacked should not act impulsively. He should remain calm and not react rashly which likely would cause more problems.

6. 1. He saw foolish people (folly) sitting in places or positions of authority or respect (Ecclesiastes 10:6–7). Sometimes fools rise to positions of authority without possessing the wisdom to fulfill their responsibilities.

   2. He saw rich men occupying humble places in society (Ecclesiastes 10:6).

3. He saw men of common origin (slaves) rise to exalted positions and people of noble birth (princes) living common lives (Ecclesiastes 10:7).

7. a. 1. Wisdom doesn't eliminate all risks in life (Ecclesiastes 10:8–9).
   2. Wisdom should be exercised even during the planning stage so that human energy is not wasted (Ecclesiastes 10:10).
   3. Exercising wisdom protects work from ongoing mistakes that could rob the project of ultimate success (Ecclesiastes 10:11). A wise man will both plan his work and protect his work.

   b. 1. A fool's speech is full of folly and devoid of sound reasoning (Ecclesiastes 10:13).
   2. A fool's speech is voluminous; he often talks too much (Ecclesiastes 10:14). A fool's speech often indicates he thinks he knows the future. Foolish people, trying to impress or profit from others, often make bold declarative statements about what will happen in the future. Psychic readers, mystics, and some within the media are examples of this sort of folly.

   c. 1. A wise man carefully chooses his words (Ecclesiastes 5:2).
   2. A wise man's speech is gracious (Ecclesiastes 10:12).
   3. A wise man's words motivate others (Ecclesiastes 12:11).
   4. A wise man's words are truthful and spoken in love (Ephesians 4:15).
   5. A wise man's speech is free from filthiness or silly talk (Ephesians 4:29; 5:4).

8. a. 1. There can be an immature king or ruler. This individual might be inexperienced because of his age or just immature in his decision-making ability.
   2. The leaders of the government abuse their positions by using their position for their own benefit (pleasure, laziness) rather than properly governing the people.

   b. 1. The king is noble.
   2. The government is responsible for its actions.

9. A house not properly maintained eventually experiences structural problems that could lead to internal problems (leaking roof, decay, etc.). In the same way, a nation that's not well governed will eventually experience internal problems (rebellion, exploitation of the poor, etc.) and crumble.

10. 1. Christians should not be shocked or surprised. Other government leaders will usually hold each other accountable (Ecclesiastes 5:8).
    2. Christians should be careful not to criticize the leaders (Ecclesiastes 10:20). The things a believer says might be quoted (or misquoted) to others.
    3. Christians should pray for those in authority (1 Timothy 2:1–3).

11. Answers will vary.

Lesson 10: Living Without Fear

1. a. The immediate context favors the need to diversify in commerce because the verses following address the uncertainty of knowing the future (Ecclesiastes 11:3–6). The phrases "you will find it" (v. 1) and "you do not know what misfortune" also support the interpretation of commercial diversification.
    b. Answers will vary, but they could include the following: An individual shouldn't invest his discretionary income in one place. Since no one knows the future, no individual can be guaranteed a future return on a particular investment. He should invest in a variety of business opportunities because some may become wise investments.

2. a. No, Jerome's interpretation is an example of an allegorical interpretation. The two illustrations in Ecclesiastes 11:3 are examples of the misfortunes man may experience, misfortunes that are beyond his control.
    b. Natural disasters (weather, fallen trees, etc.) are an inevitable part of man's existence that are beyond his control and can affect his life.

3. a. He can't expect a return ("He ... will not reap") if he takes no risks.
    b. Answers will vary.

4. 1. He doesn't know what misfortune may occur on the earth (Ecclesiastes 11:2).
    2. He doesn't know the path of the wind (Ecclesiastes 11:5).
    3. He doesn't know how bones are formed in the womb (Ecclesiastes 11:5).

4. He doesn't know the activity of God, who made all things (Ecclesiastes 11:5).

5. He doesn't know if any of his work will be rewarded (Ecclesiastes 11:6).

5. a. Jesus told Nicodemus that he needed to be born again. He expected Nicodemus, a teacher of Israel, to know what it meant to be born again.

   b. Answers will vary.

6. An individual should always be diligent in his responsibilities at work because he has no guarantee that any or all of his endeavors will be rewarded.

7. a. People should be happy and maintain a positive outlook throughout their lifetime (Ecclesiastes 11:8). They shouldn't squander any of the days God gives them because there will be a time when they will not enjoy life (v. 8, that is, old age). The young should pursue their dreams and the inclinations of their hearts, but they shouldn't lose sight of God's future judgment (Ecclesiastes 11:9). Man shouldn't allow worry to rob his joy (v. 1, "remove sorrow from your heart"). He should also remove needless pain (probably emotional) from his life so he can enjoy the life God has given him.

   b. "in them all [many years]."

8. 1. A Christian should learn to do well in God's sight (Ecclesiastes 2:26).
   2. A Christian should learn to let the past go (Philippians 3:13).
   3. A Christian should realize that worry and anxiety are sins rather than virtues (Philippians 4:6).
   4. A Christian should learn to pray rather than worry (Philippians 4:6).
   5. A Christian should discipline his mind to dwell on good things rather than potential problems that might not happen (Philippians 4:8).
   6. A Christian should surrender to God any concern about problems (1 Peter 5:7).

9. The phrase probably refers to old age because the writer has already described death as the cessation of all existence (Ecclesiastes 3:20; 6:4). The "days of darkness" are further described as being many, which is an

unlikely description for man's eternal existence.

10. 1. God has placed the reality of eternity in the hearts of all men (Ecclesiastes 3:11).
    2. God has set a limit on man's abilities to control the world around him so that he might learn to fear God (Ecclesiastes 3:14).
    3. God tests men by showing them the brevity of life (Ecclesiastes 3:18).

Lesson 11: The Purpose of Life

1. a. God's remembrance is accompanied by His willingness to act on behalf of the individual for good.
   b. Answers will vary but could include the following: Don't forget to serve the Lord when you're young, because there will be a time when you're old and tired, and you won't have the strength to do so.
   c. Answers will vary.

2. They are evil days (days of darkness) because physical infirmity makes life difficult when you're old. The hopes of youth are gone, and the future is limited from an earthly perspective. A loss of dignity often accompanies old age.

3. a. Man experiences a gradual loss of motor reflexes, resulting in trembling limbs.
   b. Man experiences tooth loss ("they are few"), and he needs to eat more easily digestible foods ("stand idle").
   c. Man's eyesight becomes weakened.
   d. Man experiences hearing loss.
   e. Man sleeps lightly, his sleep disturbed by the slightest sounds. He also tends to rise early.
   f. Man's hair becomes white.
   g. Man often hobbles as he walks.
   h. Man's sexual desire wanes.

4. a Man's spinal column.
   b. His body returns to the dust, and his spirit returns to God, who will judge man.

5. 1. He taught the people knowledge (Ecclesiastes 12:9).
   2. He meditated on the truth of God (Ecclesiastes 12:9).
   3. He organized and arranged proverbs (Ecclesiastes 12:9).
   4. He sought to make the truth acceptable (Ecclesiastes 12:10 NASB, "delightful words").
   5. He correctly wrote the truth of God (Ecclesiastes 12:10).

6. a. The wise teacher attempted to make God's truth palatable without compromising the message.
   b. A goad is a pointed rod used to urge on an animal. The Word of God should prod people toward His truth and maturity. It should prick man in those areas of his life where he has departed from the standard of God's Word.

7. The ancient tent pegs anchored the tent, and the Word of God should anchor the lives of His people. The entire tent (including the pegs) provided shelter and security for the shepherds, and the Word of God should provide spiritual shelter and security in the lives of His people.

8. a. They are given by one Shepherd (Ecclesiastes 12:11).
   b. Jehovah/God.

9. a. Everyone should fear God and obey the Word of God. This is the most important thing in life.
   b. Everyone must eventually be judged by God.

10. Answers will vary.

ADDITIONAL INSIGHTS

FINAL EXAM

Every person will eventually stand before God in judgment—the final exam. The Bible says, **And it is appointed for men to die once, but after this the judgment** (Hebrews 9:27).

May I ask you a question? *If you died today, do you know for certain you would go to heaven?* I did not ask if you're religious or a church member, nor did I ask if you've had some encounter with God—a meaningful spiritual experience. I didn't even ask if you believe in God or angels or if you're trying to live a good life. The question I *am* asking is this: *If you died today, do you know for certain you would go to heaven?*

When you die, you will stand alone before God in judgment. You'll either be saved for all eternity, or you will be separated from God for all eternity in what the Bible calls the lake of fire (Romans 14:12; Revelation 20:11–15). Tragically, many religious people who believe in God are not going to be accepted by Him when they die.

> **Many will say to Me in that day, "Lord, Lord, have we not prophesied in Your name, cast out demons in Your name, and done many wonders in Your name?" And then I will declare to them, "I never knew you; depart from Me, you who practice lawlessness!"** (Matthew 7:22–23)

God loves you and wants you to go to heaven (John 3:16; 2 Peter 3:9). If you are not sure where you'll spend eternity, you are not prepared to meet God. God wants you to know for certain that you will go to heaven.

> **Behold, now is the accepted time; behold, now is the day of salvation.** (2 Corinthians 6:2)

The words **behold** and **now** are repeated because God wants you to know that you can be saved today. You do not need to hear those terrible words, **Depart from Me ....** Isn't that great news?

Jesus himself said, **You must be born again** (John 3:7). These aren't the words of a pastor, a church, or a particular denomination. They're the words of Jesus Christ himself. You *must* be born again (saved from eternal damnation) before you die; otherwise, it will be too late when you die! You can know for certain today that God will accept you into heaven when you die.

These things I have written to you who believe in the name of the Son of God, that you may know *that you have eternal life.*

(1 John 5:13)

The phrase *you may know* means that you can know for certain before you die that you will go to heaven. To be born again, you must understand and accept four essential spiritual truths. These truths are right from the Bible, so you know you can trust them—they are not man-made religious traditions. Now, let's consider these four essential spiritual truths.

Essential Spiritual Truth

#1

The Bible teaches that you are a sinner and separated from God.

No one is righteous in God's eyes. To be righteous means to be totally without sin, not even a single act.

There is none righteous, no, not one;
There is none who understands;
There is none who seeks after God.
They have all turned aside;
They have together become unprofitable;
There is none who does good, no, not one.
(Romans 3:10–12)

...for all have sinned and fall short of the glory of God.
(Romans 3:23)

Look at the words God uses to show that all men are sinners—**none, not one, all turned aside, not one**. God is making a point: all of us are sinners. No one is good (perfectly without sin) in His sight. The reason is sin.

Have you ever lied, lusted, hated someone, stolen anything, or taken God's name in vain, even once? These are all sins.

Are you willing to admit to God that you are a sinner? If so, then tell Him right now you have sinned. You can say the words in your heart or aloud—it doesn't matter which—but be honest with God. Now check the box if you have just admitted you are a sinner.

☐ God, I admit I am a sinner in Your eyes.

Now, let's look at the second essential spiritual truth.

Essential Spiritual Truth

#2

The Bible teaches that you cannot save yourself or earn your way to heaven.

Man's sin is a very serious problem in the eyes of God. Your sin separates you from God, both now and for all eternity—unless you are born again.

For the wages of sin is death.
(Romans 6:23)

And you He made alive, who were dead in trespasses and sins.
(Ephesians 2:1)

Wages are a payment a person earns by what he or she has done. Your sin has earned you the wages of death, which means separation from God. If you die never having been born again, you will be separated from God after death.

You cannot save yourself or purchase your entrance into heaven. The Bible says that man is **not redeemed with corruptible things, like silver or gold** (1 Peter 1:18). If you owned all the money in the world, you still could not buy your entrance into heaven. Neither can you buy your way into heaven with good works.

> *For by grace you have been saved through faith, and that not of yourselves; it is the gift of God, not of works, lest anyone should boast.* (Ephesians 2:8–9)

The Bible says salvation is **not of yourselves**. It is **not of works, lest anyone should boast**. Salvation from eternal judgment cannot be earned by doing good works; it is a gift of God. There is nothing you can do to purchase your way into heaven because you are already unrighteous in God's eyes.

If you understand you cannot save yourself, then tell God right now that you are a sinner, separated from Him, and you cannot save yourself. Check the box below if you have just done that.

☐ God, I admit that I am separated from You because of my sin. I realize that I cannot save myself.

Now, let's look at the third essential spiritual truth.

Essential Spiritual Truth

#3

The Bible teaches that Jesus Christ died on the cross to pay the complete penalty for your sin and to purchase a place in heaven for you.

Jesus Christ, the sinless Son of God, lived a perfect life, died on the cross, and rose from the dead to pay the penalty for your sin and purchase a place in heaven for you. He died on the cross on your behalf, in your place, as your substitute, so you do not have to go to hell. Jesus Christ is the only acceptable substitute for your sin.

For He [God, the Father] made Him [Jesus] who knew [committed] no sin to be sin for us, that we might become the righteousness of God in Him.
(2 Corinthians 5:21)

I [Jesus] am the way, the truth, and the life. No one comes to the Father except through Me.
(John 14:6)

Nor is there salvation in any other, for there is no other name under heaven given among men by which we must be saved.
(Acts 4:12)

Jesus Christ is your only hope and means of salvation. Because you are a sinner, you cannot pay for your sins, but Jesus paid the penalty for your sins by dying on the cross in your place. Friend, there is salvation in no one else—not angels, not some religious leader, not even your religious good works. No religious act such as baptism, confirmation, or joining a church can save you. There is no other way, no other name that can save you. Only Jesus Christ can save you. You must be saved by accepting Jesus Christ's substitutionary sacrifice for your sins, or you will be lost forever.

Do you see clearly that Jesus Christ is the only way to God in heaven? If you understand this truth, tell God that you understand, and check the box below.

☐ God, I understand that Jesus Christ died to pay the penalty for my sin. I understand that His death on the cross was the only acceptable sacrifice for my sin.

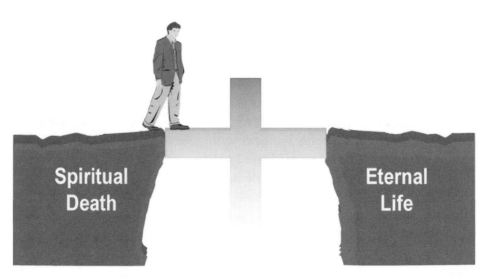

Essential Spiritual Truth

#4

By faith, you must trust in Jesus Christ alone for eternal life and call upon Him to be your Savior and Lord.

Many religious people admit they have sinned. They believe Jesus Christ died for the sins of the world, but they are not saved. Why? Thousands of moral, religious people have never completely placed their faith in Jesus Christ *alone* for eternal life. They think they must believe in Jesus Christ as a real person and do good works to earn their way to heaven. They are not trusting Jesus Christ alone. To be saved, you must trust in Jesus Christ *alone* for eternal life. Look what the Bible teaches about trusting Jesus Christ alone for salvation.

> *Believe on the Lord Jesus Christ, and you will be saved.*
> (Acts 16:31)

> *...that if you confess with your mouth the Lord Jesus and believe in your heart that God has raised Him from the dead, you will be saved. For with the heart one believes unto righteousness, and with the mouth confession is made unto salvation.... For there is no distinction between Jew and Greek, for the same Lord over all is rich to all who call upon Him. For "whoever calls on the name of the Lord shall be saved.*
> (Romans 10:9–10, 12–13)

Do you see what God is saying? To be saved or born again, you must trust Jesus Christ *alone* for eternal life. Jesus Christ paid for your complete salvation. Jesus said, **It is finished!** (John 19:30). Jesus paid for your salvation completely when He shed His blood on the cross for your sin.

If you believe that God resurrected Jesus Christ (proving God's acceptance of Jesus as a worthy sacrifice for man's sin) and you are willing to confess Jesus Christ as your Savior and Lord (master of your life), you will be saved.

Friend, right now God is offering you the greatest gift in the world. God wants to give you the *gift* of eternal life, the *gift* of His complete forgiveness for all your sins, and the *gift* of His unconditional acceptance into heaven when you die. Will you accept His free gift now, right where you are?

Are you unsure how to receive the gift of eternal life? Let me help you. Do you remember that I said you needed to understand and accept four essential spiritual truths? First, you admitted you are a sinner. Second, you admitted you were separated from God because of your sin and you could not save yourself. Third, you realized that Jesus Christ is the only way to heaven—no other name can save you.

Now, you must trust that Jesus Christ died once and for all to save your lost soul. Just take God at His word—He will not lie to you! This is the kind of simple faith you need to be saved. If you would like to be saved right now, right where you are, offer this prayer of simple faith to God. Remember, the words must come from your heart.

God, I am a sinner and deserve to go to hell. Thank You, Jesus, for dying on the cross for me and for purchasing a place in heaven for me. I believe You are the Son of God and You are able to save me right now. Please forgive me for my sin and take me to heaven when I die. I invite You into my life as Savior and Lord, and I trust You alone for eternal life. Thank You for giving me the gift of eternal life. Amen.

If, in the best way you know how, you trusted Jesus Christ alone to save you, then God just saved you. He said in His Holy Word, ***But as many as received Him, to them He gave the right to become the children of God*** (John 1:12). It's that simple. God just gave you the gift of eternal life by faith. You have just been born again, according to the Bible.

You will not come into eternal judgment, and you will not perish in the lake of fire—you are saved forever! Read this verse carefully and let it sink into your heart.

> *Most assuredly, I say to you, he who hears My word and believes in Him who sent Me has everlasting life, and shall not come into judgment, but has passed from death into life.*
> (John 5:24)

Now, let me ask you a few more questions.

According to God's holy Word (John 5:24), not your feelings, what kind of life did God just give you? _____

What two words did God say at the beginning of the verse to assure you that He is not lying to you? _____ _____

Are you going to come into eternal judgment? ☐ YES ☐ NO

Have you passed from spiritual death into life? ☐ YES ☐ NO

Friend, you've just been born again. You just became a child of God.

To help you grow in your new Christian life, we would like to send you some Bible study materials. To receive these helpful materials free of charge, e-mail your request to **info@LamplightersUSA.org.**

Spiritual Death

Eternal Life

Appendix

Level 1 (Basic Training)
Student Workbook

To begin, familiarize yourself with the Lamplighters' *Leadership Training and Development Process* (see graphic on page 118). Notice there are two circles: a smaller, inner circle and a larger, outer circle. The inner circle shows the sequence of weekly meetings beginning with an Open House, followed by an 8–14 week study, and concluding with a clear presentation of the gospel (Final Exam). The outer circle shows the sequence of the Intentional Discipleship training process (Leading Studies, Training Leaders, Multiplying Groups). As participants are transformed by God's Word, they're invited into a discipleship training process that equips them in every aspect of the intentional disciple-making ministry.

The Level 1 training (Basic Training) is *free*, and the training focuses on two key aspects of the training: 1) how to prepare a life-changing Bible study (ST-A-R-T) and 2) how to lead a life-changing Bible study (10 commandments). The training takes approximately 60 minutes to complete, and you complete it as an individual or collectively as a small group (preferred method) by inserting an extra week between the Final Exam and the Open House.

To begin your training, go to www.LamplightersUSA.org to register yourself or your group. A Lamplighters' Certified Trainer will guide you through the entire Level 1 training process. After you have completed the training, you can review as many times as you like.

When you have completed the Level 1 training, please consider completing the Level 2 (Advanced) training. Level 2 training will equip you to reach more people for Christ by learning how to train new leaders and by showing you how to multiply groups. You can register for additional training at www. LamplightersUSA.org.

Intentional Discipleship

Training & Development Process

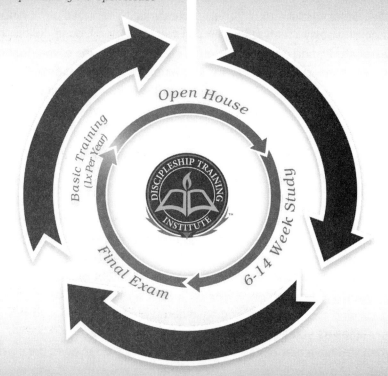

3. Multiplying Groups

The "5 Steps" for Starting
New Groups
The Audio Training Library (ATL)
The Importance of the Open House

1. Leading Studies

ST-A-R-T
10 Commandments
Solving All Group Problems

Open House

Basic Training
(1x Per Year)

DISCIPLESHIP TRAINING INSTITUTE

6-14 Week Study

Final Exam

2. Training Leaders

Four-fold ministry of a leader
The Three Diagnostic Questions

The 2P's for recruiting new leaders
The three stages of leadership training

How to Prepare a
Life-Changing Bible Study
ST-A-R-T

Step 1: _____ and _____.

    Pray specifically for the group members and yourself as you study God's
Word. Ask God (_____) to give each group member
a rich time of personal Bible study, and thank (_____) God for
giving you a desire to invest in the spiritual advancement of each other.

Step 2: _____ the _____.

    Answer the questions in the weekly lessons without looking at the

_____ _____.

Step 3: _____and _____.

    Review the Leader's Guide, and _____ every truth you missed when
you originally did your lesson. Record the answers you missed with a
_____ _____ so you'll know what you missed.

Step 4: _____ _____.

    Calculate the specific amount of time _____ _____ to
spend on each question and write the start time next to each one in the
_____ using a _____.

How to Lead a Life-Changing Bible Study

10 COMMANDMENTS

1	2	3
4	5	6
7	8	9
	10	

Lamplighters' 10 Commandments are proven small group leadership principles that have been used successfully to train hundreds of believers to lead life-changing, intentional discipleship Bible studies.

Essential Principles for Leading Intentional Discipleship Bible Studies

1. The 1st Commandment: The _____ Rule.
   The Leader-Trainer should be in the room _____ minutes before the class begins.

2. The 2nd Commandment: The _____-_____ Rule.
   Train the group that it is okay to _____, but they should never be _____.

3. The 3rd Commandment: The _____ Rule.
   _____, _____, _____ ask for _____ to _____ the _____, _____, and _____ the questions. The Leader-Trainer, however, should always _____ the questions to control the _____ of the study.

4. The 4th Commandment: The ____:____ Rule.
   _____ the Bible study on time and _____ the study on time _____ _____. No exceptions!

5. The 5th Commandment: The _____ Rule.
   Train the group participants to _____ on God's Word for answers to life's questions.

1	2	3
4 **59:59**	5	6
7	8	9
	10	

6. The 6th Commandment: The _____ Rule.
   Deliberately and progressively _____ _____ participants into the group discussion over a period of time.

7. The 7th Commandment: The _____ _____ Rule.
   _____ the participants to get _____ the answers to the questions, not just _____ or _____ ones.

8. The 8th Commandment: The _____ Rule.
   _____ the group discussion so you _____ the lesson _____ _____ and give each question _____ _____.

9. The 9th Commandment: The _____-_____ Rule.
   Don't let the group members talk about _____
   _____, _____ _____, or
   _____ _____.

10. The 10th Commandment: The _____ Rule.
    _____ God to change lives, including _____.

Choose your next study from any of the following titles:

- Joshua 1-9
- Joshua 10-24
- Judges 1-10
- Judges 11-21
- Ruth/Esther
- Jonah/Habakkuk
- Nehemiah
- Proverbs 1-9
- Proverbs 10-31
- Ecclesiastes
- John 1-11
- John 12-21
- Acts 1-12
- Acts 13-28

- Romans 1-8
- Romans 9-16
- Galatians
- Ephesians
- Philippians
- Colossians
- 1 & 2 Thessalonians
- 1 Timothy
- 2 Timothy
- Titus/Philemon
- Hebrews
- James
- 1 Peter
- 2 Peter/Jude

Additional Bible studies and sample lessons are available online.

For audio introductions on all Bible studies, visit us online at www.Lamplightersusa.org.

Looking to begin a new group?
The Lamplighters Starter Kit includes:

- 8 James Bible Study Guides
  (students purchase their own books)
- 25 Welcome Booklets
- 25 Table Tents
- 25 Bible Book Locator Bookmarks
- 50 Final Exam Tracts
- 50 Invitation Cards

For a current listing of live and online discipleship training
events, or to register for discipleship training, go to
www.LamplightersUSA.org/training.